D0436775

THE SCORPION'S STING

Also by James Oakes

Freedom National: The Destruction of
Slavery in the United States, 1861–1865

The Radical and the Republican: Frederick Douglass,
Abraham Lincoln, and the Triumph of Antislavery Politics

Slavery and Freedom: An Interpretation of the Old South

The Ruling Race: A History of American Slaveholders

THE
SCORPION'S STING

Antislavery and the
Coming of the Civil War

JAMES OAKES

W. W. NORTON & COMPANY

New York   London

Frontispiece: In this 1862 image the metaphor of the scorpion's sting, popular before the Civil War, is reimagined to apply to the military conditions of the moment. The cotton South is the scorpion, now surrounded by the Union army moving from the west and the Union navy along the Gulf coast. Realizing the hopelessness of its situation, it prepares to commit suicide by stinging itself.

For information about permission to reproduce selections from this book,
write to Permissions, W. W. Norton & Company, Inc.,
500 Fifth Avenue, New York, NY 10110

For information about special discounts for bulk purchases, please contact
W. W. Norton Special Sales at specialsales@wwnorton.com or 800-233-4830

Manufacturing by Courier Westford
Book design by Helene Berinsky
Production manager: Devon Zahn

ISBN 978-0-393-23993-5

W. W. Norton & Company, Inc.
500 Fifth Avenue, New York, N.Y. 10110
www.wwnorton.com

W. W. Norton & Company Ltd.
Castle House, 75/76 Wells Street, London W1T 3QT

1 2 3 4 5 6 7 8 9 0

For my teachers

Contents

THE SCORPION'S STING

At Stake

THE MEN AND WOMEN who struggled to abolish slavery were not counting on a war to get the job done. Of course they knew about military emancipation. Freeing slaves as a "military necessity" in wartime was an ancient practice, familiar to the histories of Greece and Rome, the African continent, Latin America, and the United States. But abolitionists and antislavery politicians were not planning for a war so that the U.S. Army could sweep through the South emancipating as it went. If there was a war or rebellion, the federal government would certainly have the power to free slaves as a military necessity. But slavery's opponents most often put their faith in an entirely different program designed to bring about the "ultimate extinction" of slavery. They would withdraw all federal support for slavery, surround the South with a "cordon of freedom," pressuring the slave states to abolish the institution on their own. "Like a scorpion girt by fire," antislavery activists argued, slavery would eventually sting itself to death. When the slave states seceded from the Union beginning in late 1860, they were not fleeing the prospect of military emancipation, they were hoping to avoid the scorpion's sting.

By specifying exactly what slavery's opponents hoped to accomplish—the burden of chapter one—we can see more clearly why none of the secession-winter proposals for sectional compromise succeeded in averting war. The second chapter does something similar, but from a different angle. It begins by clarifying the definition of *slavery*—which Americans understood to mean property rights in human beings—so that we can better understand what a debate over slavery might have looked like. This in turn makes it easier to see why disputes over seemingly marginal issues—slavery in the territories, fugitive slaves, or abolition in Washington, D.C.—were always driven by an underlying conflict over the right versus the wrong of "property in man." New World slavery was also "racial" in that it restricted enslavement to sub-Saharan Africans and their descendants, a broad constellation of human beings widely supposed to constitute a distinct "race." This made it impossible to argue about slavery without arguing about racial equality. Chapter three recovers that argument. Together these three chapters highlight the depth and significance of the Republican Party's threat to slavery on the eve of the Civil War.

That threat did not include military emancipation, at least not before the secession crisis. By surveying the long history of military emancipation in the United States, chapter four demonstrates that freeing slaves in wartime was a mainstream idea whose origins lay well outside the abolitionist movement. This last point requires some elaboration.

———————

THE EMANCIPATION PROCLAMATION occupies center stage in most accounts of slavery's destruction. It's easy to see why. Issued on January 1, 1863, at the midpoint of the Civil War, the proclamation provides a convenient climax to a large and dramatic story. It transformed the nature of the war. It altered Union policy on the ground in the southern states. It was an attempt to use military emancipation not simply as a weapon of war but as a means of destroying slavery. Although military emancipation had been commonplace in human history, including American history, it was not at all common to proclaim *all* slaves free as a military necessity. It's no wonder we spend so much time thinking about Lincoln's proclamation.

But like an exploded supernova, the Emancipation Proclamation has become a gravitational force so dense that other important antislavery policies—state abolition and the Thirteenth Amendment—too often disappear into the black hole of military emancipation. Interpretations of slavery's demise pull us almost irresistibly toward January 1, 1863. Lincoln idolaters sometimes write as if he were destined to free the slaves from the time he was a young man. Skeptics, recoiling from the excesses of Great Man History, have instead constructed what might be called a Reluctance Narrative that, ironically, depends on the very same end point—universal military emancipation. Lincoln worshippers posit a "political genius" who skillfully prepared the ground for the proclamation, a man so exquisitely attuned to the movement of public opinion that he alone could sense the precise moment when the American people were at last ready to accept a policy of universal military emancipation. Skeptics, by contrast, start from the premise that Lincoln could have or should have issued the Emancipation Proclamation as soon as the war started in April 1861. The skeptical narrative then sweeps through the events of the next twenty months, stopping at the various points along the way to show how every law passed by Congress and every order issued by Lincoln failed to measure up to the standard of universal military emancipation, and from that succession of failures the skeptics infer a reluctance to emancipate.

To say that these interpretations put too much emphasis on Lincoln's proclamation is not to deny the importance of the origins and evolution of universal military emancipation. But military emancipation turned out to be a brutal and ineffective way to destroy slavery. No matter how aggressively implemented, military emancipation could not reach the majority of slaves, nor could it guarantee the permanent freedom of those it did reach. All along, Lincoln had higher hopes for the cordon of freedom leading to the eventual abolition of slavery on a state-by-state basis. But that didn't work either, and in the end the complete destruction of slavery required yet a third policy—a thirteenth amendment to the Constitution.[1]

Lincoln did not dream up the idea of state-by-state abolition on his own. The North had abolished slavery that way in the late eighteenth century. But a concerted federal policy designed to get the southern states to abolish slavery—that idea came from the abolitionists. When they began petitioning Congress to shift the bias of federal policy away from slavery and toward freedom, they demanded things like the abolition of slavery in Washington, D.C., a ban on slavery in the territories, state rather than federal enforcement of the fugitive-slave clause, the suppression of the Atlantic slave trade, and the withdrawal of all federal support for slavery on the high seas. This set of policies became the centerpiece of the radical antislavery agenda. Wartime emancipation imposed by the military was always an option, but nobody thought it was a particularly good way to abolish slavery. John Quincy Adams first speculated that it could be done, and others—Joshua Giddings, for example—agreed that slavery could be abolished by means of military emancipation. But it wasn't the way they wanted to end slavery. The American Antislavery Society never advocated military emancipation as a means of freeing all the slaves. It was not part of the Liberty Party platform. The Free Soilers didn't talk about it. By the mid-1850s local Republican Party organizations across the North were adopting resolutions urging the federal government to implement many of the policies first advocated by antislavery radicals, but their resolutions never included military emancipation.

Having been elected on a promise to put slavery on a course of ultimate extinction by surrounding it with a cordon of freedom, Abraham Lincoln and the Republicans proceeded to do just that. In the very first regular session of Congress over which they had control—between December 1861 and July 1862—Lincoln and the Republicans abolished slavery in Washington, D.C., banned slavery from the territories, stopped enforcing the fugitive-slave clause in the northern states, signed a treaty with Great Britain to suppress the Atlantic slave trade, and required the new state of West Virginia to abolish slavery as a condition for admission to the Union. Republicans took advantage of the war by putting enormous pressure on the Border States to abolish slavery on their own. The policy was, to a remarkable degree, successful. Between 1804 and 1860 not a single state abolished slavery, but by the time the Civil War ended six more states had done so.

But much of that history is obscured by the nearly exclusive focus on military emancipation and its apotheosis, the Emancipation Proclamation. This is one of the points I want to make in these pages: the scorpion's sting was the radical policy, born of the abolitionist movement, adopted in principle by the Republican Party in the 1850s, and substantially implemented during the first year of the Civil War.

And yet Republicans began threatening military emancipation during the secession crisis when war suddenly seemed imminent, and they began freeing slaves as a military necessity shortly after the war began. At first glance this seems odd. Not only were antislavery radicals not counting on a war, they did not believe a war was necessary to get slavery abolished. When those advocating abolition raised the prospect of military emancipation, it was usually to dismiss the likelihood of secession. They assumed that the South would never secede because that would mean war and with war came military emancipation. But this was a background assumption, something people took for granted because freeing slaves was what belligerents always did during wars. Far from being a distinctively radical idea, military emancipation was a conventional proposition, accepted by radicals and conservatives alike, a policy so deeply embedded in American history that it could be assumed without being asserted.

Secession and war suddenly brought into the foreground what had always been there in the background. Threats of military emancipation poured forth from Republican presses all through the secession crisis and within a few months after Fort Sumter Republican lawmakers and a Republican administration began freeing slaves as a military necessity. At first they stayed within the familiar precedents for wartime emancipation by offering freedom only to slaves who came within Union lines from areas in rebellion or from rebel masters. As they came to realize how weak Unionism was in the South, how loyal the slaves were, and how much resistance there was to abolition in the Border States, however, Republicans moved closer to adopting a policy of *universal* military emancipation. With the Second Confiscation Act of July 1862, as fully implemented by the Emancipation Proclamation several months later, universal military emancipation took its place alongside state abolition as a means of destroying slavery in the South.

Nobody could have predicted this would happen. Everybody knew about military emancipation, but few imagined that it would become as important as it did by 1863, and there were no precedents in American history for universal military emancipation. Instead, federal antislavery policy evolved in unforeseen ways over the course of the war, an evolution driven by events on the ground in the slave states, by shifts in national politics, and by the contingencies of war itself. When the fighting began, few Northerners thought that slavery would prove so durable or that the slaveholders would put up such a ferocious fight to save it. The Republicans were confident that slaves would run for their freedom to Union lines; slaves always did that. But the slaves understood better than the Republicans how many roadblocks their masters could throw down in the way, and in any case federal policy makers were not prepared to handle the number of slaves who overcame the obstacles and made it to Union lines. Then, too, there were the uncertainties of the war itself. A few insiders might have been able to predict that Robert E. Lee would prove so formidable on the field of battle, but nobody thought that about Ulysses Grant and none foresaw that George B. McClellan would prove so inadequate or that somebody named Joshua Chamberlain would inspire his men to hold on to Little Round Top on the second day at Gettysburg. Few people imagined that Abraham Lincoln would turn out to be such an effective president. Everybody knew in 1861 that the fate of slavery hung in the balance, but nobody could have predicted that under the intense pressure of war six states would abolish slavery, that military emancipation would be universalized, but that neither would be enough to destroy slavery. Hardly anybody in 1861 imagined that the Constitution would have to be rewritten for slavery to be destroyed, and nobody knew, as late as the summer of 1864, whether Lincoln and the Republicans would hold on to Congress and the presidency long enough, and in large enough numbers, to get the Thirteenth Amendment passed.

It's possible, even tempting, to make the abolition of slavery seem as inevitable as the war itself can be made to seem, to construct a narrative arc in which each different antislavery policy led inexorably to its logical successor. But history doesn't work that way. The Republicans hated slavery and intended to destroy it, but intentions don't make outcomes inevitable. After all, the slaveholders intended to preserve slavery, and that didn't ensure slavery's survival. To show how slavery was destroyed is not to show that the destruction of slavery was inevitable.

The same thing can be said of the Civil War itself. The conflict was so long, so destructive, and so murderous that historians understandably spend a lot of their time considering the various proposals for sectional compromise that might have worked but for some reason or other did not. This sustained search for the alternatives to what happened is often driven by a deep and justifiable horror of the war that did, finally, come. It's a humane impulse, and it can be a salutary one—it keeps us on guard against the tendency to make the war seem inevitable. No account of the coming of the Civil War can afford to ignore the possibility that it might have gone some other way. But in the end the historian must explain what actually did happen and why. The war came. Compromise failed. And these chapters are a partial attempt to explain what was at stake in the sectional crisis and why the conflict over slavery had become irreconcilable. They may also help explain why an irreconcilable conflict over slavery did not make the abolition of slavery inevitable.

⇛ 1 ⇚

"Like a Scorpion Girt by Fire"

I N JANUARY 1860, during a heated debate over slavery in the House of Representatives, Pennsylvania Congressman Thaddeus Stevens explained, "in the briefest possible manner," what he considered to be the underlying principles of the Republican Party. "In my judgment," he began, "Republicanism is founded in love of universal liberty, and in hostility to slavery and oppression throughout the world. Undoubtedly, had we the legal right and the physical power, we would abolish human servitude and overthrow despotism in every land that the sun visits in its diurnal course. But we claim no such high privilege or mission," Stevens insisted. "We claim no right to interfere with the institutions of foreign nations, or with the institutions of the sister States of this Republic. We would wish that Russia would liberate her serfs, Austria her oppressed subjects, Turkey her minions, and the South her slaves. But the law of nations gives us no authority to redress foreign grievances; and the Constitution of the United States gives us no power to interfere with the institutions of our sister States. And we do deny now, as we have ever denied, that there is any desire or intention, on the part of the Republican party, to interfere with those institutions. . . ."[1]

This was a standard disclaimer among Republicans. His radicalism notwithstanding, Thaddeus Stevens had always endorsed the federal consensus, agreeing with conservative and moderate Republicans as well as Democrats, north and south, that the national government had no power under the Constitution to abolish slavery in a state where it already existed. That disclaimer is important because it tells us what Republicans would *not* do to undermine slavery, but it does not tell us what they *would* do. And so, Stevens continued, "[W]hile we claim no power to interfere with the institution in the States, yet where the law of no State operates, and where the responsibility of government is thrown on Congress, we do claim the power to regulate and the right to abolish slavery. . . ." Which places were these? Stevens elaborated: "[T]he Territories, the District of Columbia, the navy-yards, and the arsenals have no legislative bodies but Congress, or those granted by Congress; and it is our purpose to provide in the exercise of our legislative duty, for preventing the extension of slavery into free soil under the jurisdiction of this General Government, or any extension of slavery upon this continent."

That next-to-last phrase—the part about "preventing the extension of slavery into free soil"—was a thinly veiled promise to inhibit the recapture of fugitive slaves in northern states where slavery was illegal. It prompted Virginia

Congressman Sherrard Clemens to ask Stevens whether he supported the Fugitive Slave Act of 1850. Stevens answered that he had voted against the law, that he favored either its repeal or its modification, that in his "political" opinion it was "unconstitutional"—though as long as it remained on the books, Stevens added, "I shall not resist its execution."

Clemens then asked Stevens to confirm a statement he had once made, to the effect that the purpose of the Republican Party "was to encircle the slave States of this Union with free States as a cordon of fire, and that slavery, like a scorpion, would sting itself to death. I ask the gentleman if he did not make that remark, or something like it?"

Stevens made a brief, sarcastic reply to the effect that if he had made such a remark, "it is on the books."

Not satisfied, Clemens pressed the issue. "I put to him respectfully this question . . ." Clemens said, "if his policy is carried out, whether to-day, to-morrow, or fifty years hence; if not a single new slave State is admitted into the Union; if slavery is abolished in the District of Columbia, in the Territories, in the arsenals, dockyards, and forts; if, in addition to that, his party grasps the power of the Presidency, with the patronage attached to it . . . —whether, if he did all this, would he not carry out the full extent of the remarks which he made, that he would have slavery surrounded like a camp in a prairie or a scorpion with fire, and if it would not sting itself to death?"

"I do not know," Stevens answered dismissively, "not being a prophet. [Laughter.]"[2]

Stevens was being coy. Clemens was not asking him to issue a prophecy, to predict what would actually happen if

Republican policies were implemented. He wanted to know if the doom of slavery was what Stevens *hoped* for, what he and his fellow Republicans *anticipated* would happen, should they succeed in surrounding the South with a cordon of freedom. That was the point of the metaphor about the scorpion—eventually, it would kill itself—and nobody knew that better than Thaddeus Stevens. For by 1860 the scorpion's sting had become a popular literary device for capturing the process by which the opponents of slavery expected it to die. Although the federal government would do all it could to encourage them, the states themselves would eventually abolish their own slave systems. The sooner the better.

In January 1847, in their fifteenth annual report, the board of managers of the Massachusetts Anti-Slavery Society pointed to the various ways in which slavery was becoming more and more unacceptable in polite society, at least in England. "When public sentiment is such in the British Islands, that no Slaveholder can be received into any pulpit or at any communion table," the report declared, when "an enlightened public opinion" no longer tolerates proslavery sentiments, when they are excluded from every venue of public or private life, then "the circle of fire which has already been kindled around the scorpion will grow hotter and hotter, and close nearer and nearer, until it will be compelled to bury its sting in its own brain, and rid the world, by a blessed suicide, of its monstrous existence."[3]

The image of the scorpion's sting soon spread far beyond the confines of New England abolitionism, and by the mid-1850s it was popular among antislavery politicians across the

North. "The Republican party does not wish to interfere in the internal government or social institutions of the slave States, but merely to place around them a cordon of free States," Anson Burlingame explained in 1856. "Then," he added, "this *horrible* system will die of inanition; or, *like the scorpion, seeing no means of escape, sting itself to death.*"[4] Even colonizationists invoked the imagery to support their program. In 1861, writing "as an Abolitionist and a Republican," James Redpath proposed the construction of a colony of former slaves on the Caribbean island-nation of Haiti. Colonization would do two things, Redpath argued. It would demonstrate "the capacity of the race for self-government," and it would also "carry out the programme of the ablest intellects of the Republican Party,—of surrounding the Southern States with a cordon of free labor, within which, like a scorpion girded by fire, Slavery must inevitably die."[5]

For those who opposed slavery by political means, the scorpion's sting perfectly captured their program of abolition. Under normal circumstances the federal government would not—could not—go into any southern state and directly abolish slavery. The Constitution did not allow that. But the government could create the conditions that would lead the slave states to abolish slavery on their own. Indeed, the government should have been doing this all along. We should never have annexed Texas, James Freeman Clarke declared in 1859, nor should we have repealed the Missouri Compromise. We should have adopted the Wilmot Proviso and rejected the Fugitive Slave Act. Defeated "on these points," Clarke explained, the slave power "would have ceased from its aggressions; the lovers of Freedom at the South would have been encouraged; the Border States would have been led to take measures for emancipation. Gradually, peacefully, joyfully the cause of Freedom would have grown strong, that of Slavery weak—until, at last, surrounded by the hosts of Free labor, by emigrants from the North, by invading light and advancing religion; hemmed in by all this illumination and warmth, like the scorpion girt with fire, it would have turned its sting against itself."[6]

Clarke was commenting on John Brown's raid on Harper's Ferry, explaining why the struggle over slavery ought never to have reached such violent extremes. The war with Mexico, the lawlessness in Kansas, the decades-long "border wars" along the Mason-Dixon Line and the Ohio River, the inflammatory dragging of fugitives through the streets of northern cities, and now John Brown's failed attempt to get up a slave insurrection—none of this violence was necessary, Clarke argued, none of it would have happened, had the government instead pursued a consistent policy of containing slavery within a "cordon of freedom" so that abolition could be achieved "gradually, peacefully, joyfully."

We can debate back and forth whether a cordon would have worked in the absence of a war, and I can posit a variety of hypothetical scenarios in which it fails miserably or succeeds brilliantly. As always with such scenarios, had things been different, things would have been different. But in the end this counterfactual exercise is a distraction because the historical significance of the cordon of freedom does not depend on the answer to an unanswerable question. The policy of surrounding the South and squeezing slavery to death was important, if for no other reason, because it was the project to which Republicans were committed when they secured the presidency in 1860 and took control of Congress in 1861. And as William Freehling has amply demonstrated—it was not merely the proposed ban on slavery in the western territories, but the larger threat of slow strangulation by encirclement, that provoked the southern states to secede from the Union, thereby leading to Civil War. It made the sectional struggle over slavery irreconcilable.

ACCORDING TO THE Republican governor of Indiana, Oliver P. Morton, the central doctrine of his party was "to reinstate the ancient idea that slavery is sectional and freedom national; that slavery, being a domestic institution, can only exist by local law."[7] This principle was forthrightly proclaimed in the Republican Party's 1860 platform. The "normal condition of all the territory of the United States is that of freedom." In those areas, where no state governments existed and hence no state laws had created slavery, the Constitution alone was sovereign. Because the Constitution proclaims that "no person shall . . . be deprived of life, liberty or property, without due process of law," the federal government was obliged to assume universal freedom in all areas under its direct jurisdiction. Convinced that these were principles embraced by the Founders, Republicans denounced what they called "the new dogma that the Constitution, of its own force, carries slavery into any or all territories of the United States." Slavery was a state institution and only a state institution. It had no extraterritorial reach, beyond the borders of the states that legalized it. Freedom was national—indeed, international; slavery was merely local.[8]

Freedom national implied a number of different antislavery policies in different parts of the country. But in the 1850s the issue that provoked the most turmoil was the expansion of slavery into the western territories, and by 1860 that was the one issue on which Republicans were unwilling to compromise. Excluding slavery from the territories was the party's line in the sand, the point beyond which it would not go. But the fact that Republicans would not abandon one policy does not mean it was the only policy to which Republicans were committed. By late 1854 anti-Nebraska conventions were popping up across northern Illinois and issuing resolutions that addressed a number of slavery-related issues. In October a Springfield meeting drafted just such a platform, affirming broad antislavery principles. "[A]s freedom is natural and slavery sectional and local," the Springfield delegates resolved, "the absence of all law upon the subject of slavery presumes the existence of a state of Freedom alone, while slavery exists only by virtue of positive law." Not surprisingly, the convention denounced Douglas's doctrine of "popular sovereignty" and argued instead that the federal government had "the right and the duty" to ban slavery from all federal territory, including all territory acquired in the future. But the delegates also defended the right of northern states to pass personal liberty laws that inhibited federal enforcement of the fugitive-slave clause. "[W]e regard the trial by jury and the writ of habeas corpus, as safeguards of personal liberty so necessary, that . . . no citizens of other states can fairly ask us to consent to their abrogation."[9] In what was billed as an "Anti-Nebraska Convention," Illinois delegates nevertheless espoused broad antislavery principles and endorsed policies that went beyond the mere restoration of the ban on slavery in the Nebraska territory.

Freedom national meant much more than keeping slavery out of Kansas. Stephen A. Douglas understood this perfectly well. In 1858, in the opening minutes of the very first of his seven famous debates with Abraham Lincoln, Douglas read from a set of resolutions passed by a local Republican organization in Aurora, Illinois. To "bring the administration of the government back to the control of first principles," the Aurora Republicans resolved "to restore Nebraska and Kansas to the position of free territories; . . . to repeal and entirely abrogate the fugitive slave law; to restrict slavery to those States in which it exists; to prohibit the admission of any more slave States into the Union; to abolish slavery in the District of Columbia; to exclude slavery from all the territories over which the general government has exclusive jurisdiction; and to resist the acquirements of any more territories unless the practice of slavery therein forever shall have been prohibited."[10]

Douglas denounced this as the "Abolition platform" of the "Black Republican" party. He dismissed the accompanying resolution in which Republicans promised not to abolish slavery in any state where it existed. All that meant, Douglas said, is that instead of marching into the slave states with guns blazing, Republicans would line up along the northern bank of the Ohio River and shoot across into Kentucky. It is worth taking a closer look at some of those policies in the "abolition" platform.

First, virtually all Republicans believed that Congress could abolish slavery in Washington, D.C. District abolition was a policy that followed logically—if not inevitably—from the Republican principle that freedom was the "normal condition" of all territory under U.S. jurisdiction. The District of Columbia was not a state. It was governed directly by Congress, and among Republicans this meant that Congress was perfectly within its power to abolish slavery. Some even said that the due process clause of the Fifth Amendment to the Constitution created a moral obligation on the part of the federal government to free all slaves under its direct jurisdiction.

For similar reasons, Republicans believed, the federal government was obliged to protect freedom rather than slavery on the high seas. This was hinted at in the 1860 platform, which denounced "the recent reopening of the African slave trade, under the cover of our national flag."[11] But the platform did not specify the new federal policies implied by this condemnation—aggressive federal prosecution of slave traders, for one; a treaty with Britain aimed at the suppression of the Atlantic slave trade, for another. For some Republicans the premise that slavery was merely local meant that Congress had the power to shut down the coastwise slave trade as well.

For most, but not all, Republicans, freedom national meant that the fugitive-slave clause of the Constitution should be enforced locally. Antislavery politicians made much of the fact that there was no enforcement provision in the clause itself, a conspicuous absence—Republicans argued—because where it appears in the Constitution the fugitive-slave clause is grouped with a number of others, all of which did contain enforcement provisions. Acting on the assumption that slavery was strictly a state institution and that states alone were constitutionally empowered to enforce the fugitive-slave clause, several northern states had passed "personal liberty laws" aimed at ensuring that accused runaways were not deprived of the due process rights to which all citizens were presumptively entitled. Even after the Supreme Court had repeatedly declared most of the personal liberty laws unconstitutional, several northern states refused to repeal them—to the consternation of even the most moderate Southerners.[12]

So long as southern slaveholders claimed the right to go into the North and enforce the slave codes of their own states, northern soil could never be genuinely free soil. The personal liberty laws were designed to change this, but there were others. Early in the nineteenth century most northern states were fairly liberal in allowing slaveholders to "sojourn" in the North. Masters could not only travel with their slaves through the free states on their way to some final destination, they were also free to bring their slaves with them into the free states for extended visits. But as sectional tensions between North and South escalated, the northern states one by one clamped down on the so-called right of sojourn. Eventually, even the most conservative states of the Midwest, states long dominated by Democrats sympathetic to the interests of southern slaveholders—even states like Illinois and Indiana—restricted the right of masters to travel with slaves in their states. By 1860 slaveholders visiting or merely passing through the North could no longer safely assume that their claim on the slaves traveling with them was secure because, according to familiar antislavery constitutional principles, slaves were automatically freed when brought into a state that had no "positive" laws protecting masters in transit with their slaves.[13]

The personal liberty laws restricting the right of southern masters to capture and return fugitives in the North, together with the laws restricting the right of sojourn, were part of a larger antislavery project aimed at encircling the South with a cordon of freedom. Opponents of slavery wanted desperately to make northern soil *free* soil, but they also wanted to make the territories and the oceans free as well. The controversy over slavery in the territories needs to be understood in this context.

The policy to which Republicans were most adamantly committed was the prohibition against the expansion of slavery into the western territories along with its logical corollary—the refusal to admit any new slave states into the Union. Slavery's westward expansion was clearly the most contentious issue from the mid-1840s onward, the one that most sorely aggravated sectional tensions. For Republicans in 1860, excluding slavery from the territories was indeed the line in the sand, but it was also—to employ a different cliché—the tip of the iceberg. Beneath the surface was a larger project, slavery's "ultimate extinction."

How would "ultimate extinction" ultimately work? What would it take to make the scorpion sting itself and die? Only occasionally did an individual Republican—usually a radical like Thaddeus Stevens or Charles Sumner—lay out the broad antislavery agenda of the party. But if you read enough Republican speeches and editorials, it's possible to reconstruct the party's scenario for gradual abolition.

It looked something like this. Once the northern states stopped enforcing the fugitive-slave clause, the deterioration of slavery in the Border States would accelerate. The annual flight of slaves into the North, from Delaware to Missouri, would become a flood tide that southern masters would be unable to stop. The only way for Border State slaveholders to prevent a mass exodus of fugitives would be to sell off their slaves to the cotton states, or pack up and leave. But masters hoping to avoid the unprecedented insecurity of slavery in the Border States would be denied the option of carrying their slaves into the territories. Instead, each new territory would enter the Union as a free state. Meanwhile, the Border States—depleted of slaves and therefore slaveholders—would begin abolishing slavery on their own. This was not an entirely unreasonable expectation on the eve of the Civil War. Slavery had all but disappeared in Delaware and half of Maryland's black population was already free. As this process advanced, the number of free states would grow steadily as the number of slave states inexorably declined, shifting the balance of power in national politics from slavery to freedom. All it would take was a shift from slavery to freedom in half a dozen states to make an abolition amendment feasible.

Most antislavery advocates thought abolition would proceed on a state-by-state basis. As slavery became concentrated in the states of the Deep South, its intrinsic weaknesses would become more and more intolerable. Slavery's economic vitality could no longer be sustained by steady infusions of fresh western soil. The borders of free soil would press ever closer to the edges of the cotton states—and the process of slavery's internal dissolution that had already taken place in the Border States would commence in the Deep South. The slaves, restless and increasingly anxious for their freedom, now pent up and concentrated in the cotton belt, would become rebellious and even revolutionary. As cotton lands were exhausted and outlets for expansion were closed off, the already sickly slave economy would begin to collapse. The value of slave property would dwindle to nothing. The vise-like grip of the slaveholding minority within the southern states would give way as the slaveless white majorities asserted themselves, unwilling to be dragged down with slavery's sinking ship. A homegrown antislavery party would finally emerge in the heart of slave country. The end would come when the slaveholders themselves awakened to the realization that their own future prosperity could only be ensured by shifting to free labor. Then the slave states would abolish slavery on their own. The scorpion, having stung itself, would die.

No one could be sure how long it would be before slavery was ultimately extinguished. Thaddeus Stevens once predicted that gradual abolition would take about twenty-five years. Owen Lovejoy, the abolitionist congressman from Illinois, was prepared to be a bit more generous. If it takes twenty-five years, that's fine, Lovejoy said; if it takes fifty years, so be it—so long as the process was begun immediately and was irreversible. The *Chicago Tribune* said in 1858 that "no man living" would see the end of slavery. In an offhand remark Lincoln once said that if slavery were to be abolished in the "most peaceful" and "most gradual" way possible, it might take a hundred years, but by the time he made the remark he no longer believed it could happen that way. Only once did Lincoln specify a particular timetable for gradual abolition. That was in November 1861, when, as president, he drafted a set of model proposals for gradual abolition in the loyal slave states. Lincoln offered states the option of completing the process in as little as five years and as many as thirty-five. But if he had his way, Lincoln said, gradual abolition would begin immediately and would be completed in ten years, and the state would be punished if it tried to reverse the process.

However long it took, gradual abolition was conceived as a peaceful process, thoroughly constitutional because undertaken by the slave states themselves, though with the support of the federal government. Over and over again antislavery politicians portrayed the cordon of freedom as the nonviolent alternative to the kind of swift, brutal military emancipation that would be imposed should the South provoke a war by seceding from the Union. Slavery "will be overthrown," William Seward predicted in 1855, "either peacefully or lawfully, under this Constitution," or by means of a violent struggle in which "the slaveholders would perish." But a violent struggle was neither necessary nor inevitable. "The change can be made now without violence," Seward argued, "by the agency of the ballot-box." But wasn't there something irreducibly violent in the metaphor of the scorpion's sting, especially as Seward invoked it? Slavery "must die," he said, "like the scorpion, by the poison of its own sting" or "as a poisoned rat dies of rage in its own hole." But when Seward spoke of slavery as dying "without violence," he meant without armed force. The scorpion's suicidal sting may seem far removed from nonviolence, but it wasn't war.[14]

Carl Schurz likewise insisted that a cordon of freedom around the South was the peaceful path to abolition, the

preferred alternative to bloody, wartime military emancipation. "[I]f slavery cannot thrive, unless it be allowed to
expand," he declared, "pen it up!" No doubt Southerners
would complain bitterly about this. "They will predict fearful things," he said. But eventually, realizing their options,
Southerners would most likely calm down because if they
did not, the consequences would be much worse. "Now, this
is your choice," Schurz warned. "Either govern this Republic as citizens on perfectly equal terms, or, as an arrogant
slaveholding aristocracy, submit to the doom of a hopeless
minority. Here is strife and disappointment—there is peace
and prosperity; choose. . . ."[15]

Schurz was confident that once Republican antislavery
policies were put in place, the peaceful process of gradual
abolition would commence. The slaveholders' arrogance
and aristocratic pride would gradually give way to their
nobler instincts and to the common sense of self-interest.
They would realize that the path to prosperity lay in free
rather than enslaved labor. Meanwhile America's reputation
in the world would rise, reflecting its proper distinction as
a beacon of liberty for all people. "This state of things will,
according to my profound conviction, be the consequence
of a consistent, peaceable, and successful anti-slavery policy,"
Schurz explained. "It will stop extravagant and unwarrant-
able claims, without interfering with constitutional rights. It
will respect the privileges of the States, but will enforce them
in favor of freedom also. It will not try to abolish slavery in
the States by Congressional interference, or by the force of
arms."[16] It was crucial to men like Seward and Schurz that the
"ring of fire" encircling the scorpion, the cordon of freedom

they promised to construct, was designed to accomplish the abolition of slavery without violence and without war.

This conviction was widespread among Republicans by the time Abraham Lincoln was elected president. In that very real sense the scorpion's sting amounted to a peace proposal—unacceptable to most southern leaders, to be sure—but understood by Republicans as the obvious alternative to the chaos and horror of war. By December 1860, few Republicans underestimated the severity of the threat to the Union, but they did find it hard to believe that the slave states would reject the alternative of peaceful, gradual abolition in favor of a war that promised swift, bloody military emancipation. It was for this reason that Republicans across the board—from antislavery radicals like Charles Sumner and Salmon P. Chase to more moderate men like Seward and Lincoln—initially urged one another to keep quiet and even to assume a conciliatory posture. By refusing to speak provocatively, by stressing that they would never directly abolish slavery in the states where slavery already existed, Republicans hoped to limit the scope of secession. This conciliatory posture was perfectly sincere—the conciliators were anything but frauds.

But they were clearly mistaken. No amount of conciliation could conceal the fact that in the wake of Abraham Lincoln's election in 1860 the conflict over slavery had become irreconcilable. No matter how often Republicans promised not to interfere with slavery in the states where it already existed, they could neither abandon nor conceal their commitment to a raft of specific policies expressly designed to put slavery on a course of ultimate extinction. There were certainly Republicans who were ready and willing to compromise, but none of the particular compromises they occasionally offered would satisfy the secessionists.

Nor could the slave states produce any compromise proposal that Republicans could tolerate. Historians who believe sectional reconciliation was still possible often draw our attention to the "reluctant confederates" of the upper South and the Unionists in the Border States. Had they been able to forge a coalition with northern Democrats and "moderates" from the Deep South and the Republican Party—maybe, just maybe, a war could have been avoided. But no such coalition could be forged because neither the most reluctant Confederates nor the most sincere southern Unionists could formulate a compromise proposal that was even remotely acceptable to the Republican Party or to the secessionists. Indeed, nothing exposes how far apart the sides were than the litany of concerns expressed by two of the South's leading moderates—John Gilmer of North Carolina and John J. Crittenden of Kentucky—two men strongly devoted to the Union, both of them with a burning desire to avoid war.

Strictly speaking, Gilmer never offered a compromise proposal. But he did, on December 10, 1860, address a series of questions to the president-elect in the hope that Lincoln's answers might allay what Gilmer called "the apprehensions of real danger and harm to them and their peculiar institution which have seized the people of my section." Lincoln's answer is important for a number of reasons, but here I want to emphasize Gilmer's questions. For his letter reveals that the "apprehensions" he ascribed to his "Southern constituency" went far beyond the fear that Republicans would exclude slavery from the western territories.[17]

"I respectfully ask," Gilmer began, "whether as President you would favor the abolition of slavery in the District of Columbia." If Gilmer was listing his questions in order of his priorities, slavery in the territories did not come first. Nor did it come second or third. Would you, he asked Lincoln, "approve of any law of Congress prohibiting the employment of Slaves in the Arsenals and Dock Yards where their location is in the Slave states?" This may sound far-fetched to us, but it was one of the policies Thaddeus Stevens had proposed the previous January. A little more than a year after Gilmer asked his question, Republican Congressman Isaac Arnold introduced a bill that would do the very thing he feared: abolish slavery on all federal property, including arsenals, fortresses, and dockyards in the southern states. Arnold called his proposal a bill "to render freedom national and slavery sectional."[18]

Gilmer's next question may seem equally unusual. Did Lincoln believe that Congress had the power to "interfere with slavery in the States" by filling federal offices in the South with opponents of slavery? Ever since Andrew Jackson had allowed his postmaster general to interdict the delivery of antislavery materials in Charleston, northern antislavery agitators had complained about the suppression of free speech in the slave states. In 1860 Republican editors were openly predicting that with Lincoln's election antislavery postmasters would be appointed and antislavery propaganda would once again begin flowing into the southern states. Gilmer worried that this would "lessen the value and usefulness of Slaves; —disturb the peace and quiet of their owners, or impair the institution of Slavery." That, of course, is precisely what Republicans hoped to do—"impair the institution of Slavery" by allowing antislavery voices as much freedom in the South as proslavery speakers enjoyed in the North, thus helping cultivate a homegrown antislavery movement in the southern states themselves. It is no wonder that Gilmer asked Lincoln for reassurance that this would not happen.

Gilmer wanted to know, "4th," whether, as president, Lincoln would veto any bill admitting a new slave state to the Union. Lincoln wasn't sure how to answer the question because he didn't see how the issue could arise. He wanted slavery banned from all the territories, and it was hard for him to imagine the circumstances in which a territory where slavery had been excluded might submit an application for statehood with a proslavery constitution. Lincoln was flummoxed by the question, but for Gilmer it was simple enough: would Lincoln oppose the admission of any new slave states to the Union? Here, too, Gilmer had every reason to worry because blocking the admission of new slave states was an essential feature of the Republican goal of reducing the influence of the slave states in national politics.

Gilmer's next question, the fifth, once again had nothing to do with slavery in the territories. Will you "enforce the fugitive slave law?" he asked. Would you "favor its repeal" or "suggest amendments impairing its efficiency?" The only honest answer Lincoln could give was that he did support amendments that—as far as southern leaders were concerned—would indeed impair the efficiency of the

fugitive-slave law. Specifically, Lincoln proposed a revision
of the 1850 Fugitive Slave Act that would guarantee the due
process rights of anyone accused of being a runaway slave.
In effect, Lincoln would accept federal enforcement of the
fugitive-slave clause in exchange for a federal guarantee of
the due process rights of accused fugitives. Lincoln's position rendered Gilmer's sixth and final question irrelevant.
Would you, the North Carolinian asked, lend your voice
and influence to "secure the repeal" of the personal liberty laws in the northern states? Lincoln's answer was vague
but it hardly mattered because he favored a federal statute
that did the same thing as many of the state statutes Gilmer
objected to.

That was it. Gilmer never even asked Lincoln whether
he favored a complete ban on the expansion of slavery, or
whether he would accept the restoration of the Missouri
Compromise. The admission of new slave states was related
to the territorial issue, but it was not the same thing. Every
other question Gilmer asked concerned very different
threats to slavery: the abolition of slavery in the District
of Columbia—which would create an antislavery island
in between two slave states; the analogous threat of creating safe antislavery harbors at federal installations across
the South; the use of patronage to fill federal offices in the
South with people opposed to slavery; federal enforcement
of the fugitive-slave clause and, conversely, state laws interfering with federal enforcement—these were the policies
regarding which Gilmer asked Lincoln for a public statement of reassurance to North Carolina voters. It was the
same set of policies to which—as both Thaddeus Stevens

and Stephen A. Douglas agreed—Republicans were in fact committed.

No doubt Gilmer didn't bother asking whether Lincoln supported a ban on slavery in the territories because everyone knew that he did, that the incoming president was "inflexible" on the matter. Yet if Gilmer believed that the territorial issue was the only one that mattered, his letter would have been a waste of time. A more reasonable conclusion is that Gilmer's letter reflected the widespread view among southern leaders that the Republican Party's opposition to slavery in the territories was only one part of a broader hostility to slavery—a hostility reflected in a number of specific antislavery policies whose combined purpose was to put slavery on a course of ultimate extinction.

The clearest indication that southern leaders were concerned about much more than a ban on slavery in the territories was the series of constitutional revisions and congressional resolutions proposed by Kentucky Senator John J. Crittenden as a solution to the secession crisis. Crittenden introduced his proposals on December 18, just before South Carolina seceded. Their most conspicuous feature was an omnibus constitutional amendment with half a dozen different articles addressing a variety of threats to slavery.

Crittenden's first proposed article, for example, would revive the Missouri Compromise line, although not the terms of the original Missouri Compromise. As it had been formulated in 1820, the compromise banned slavery in all territories north of the southern border of Missouri, except for Missouri itself. South of that line the fate of slavery was determined by popular sovereignty—that is, each territorial

legislature south of the Missouri Compromise line was free
to decide on its own whether to have slavery or not. Crittenden's proposal extended the compromise line to the California border and reinstituted the ban on slavery north of the
line. The Compromise of 1850 maintained the ban on slavery north of the 1820 line and extended popular sovereignty
to the Mexican Cession except for California. But Crittenden's amendment had a more proslavery bias—it banned
popular sovereignty and instead explicitly protected slavery
in the territories south of the line. "Slavery of the African
race" was "hereby recognized as existing," the amendment
read, "and shall not be interfered with by Congress, but shall
be protected as property by all departments of the territorial
government during its continuance." Crittenden would for
the first time introduce "slavery of the African race" into the
Constitution where it would be "protected as property" by
the federal government. This meant, for example, that if the
territorial legislatures of Arizona or New Mexico wanted to
abolish slavery, they would not be allowed to do so. In addition, Crittenden's proposal would protect slavery in all territory "hereafter acquired," all but inviting the expansion of
slavery into Cuba, Mexico, and Central America. Whatever
else this was, Illinois Republican Lyman Trumbull noted, it
was not the restoration of the Missouri Compromise for, as
he quickly pointed out, neither Congress nor the Constitution had ever "recognized" and "protected" slavery in a
territory.[19]

There were half a dozen other articles in Crittenden's
proposed constitutional amendment, none of them having
to do with slavery in the territories. Article II, for example,

would prohibit the federal government from abolishing slavery at federal installations in any of the slave states. Article III made it virtually impossible for Congress to abolish slavery in Washington, D.C.—a policy Republicans overwhelmingly supported. Many of those same Republicans also believed that the commerce clause gave Congress the power to regulate the interstate slave trade, and just about all Republicans believed that the federal government had not only the right but the moral obligation to suppress slavery on the high seas. Crittenden's proposed amendment would make both policies unconstitutional.

Article V of Crittenden's amendment explicitly empowered the federal government to enforce the fugitive-slave clause in the free states. This was a serious issue among Republicans, second only in significance to the ban on slavery in the territories.[20] But it was obviously important to Crittenden and his allies as well—his proposal would effectively criminalize a policy nearly all Republicans endorsed. The amendment would deprive the northern states of any power to determine how the fugitive-slave clause would be enforced. And as if that were not enough, the Kentucky senator wanted Congress to pass a series of resolutions declaring that the Fugitive Slave Act of 1850 was strictly constitutional, that it should not be repealed or modified, that it should instead be *strengthened* by the establishment of federal penalties for anyone interfering with the law. Crittenden also wanted Congress to issue a declaration to the effect that the personal liberty laws passed by northern states were "null and void." As modest compensation for these strenuous impositions of federal power within the northern states, Crittenden was prepared to alter the fee structure so that U.S. commissioners would be paid the same amount whether or not they ruled in favor of the master claiming a slave as a fugitive.

John J. Crittenden was devoted to the Union. He believed secession was illegal, and he wanted desperately to find some way of avoiding a terrible civil war. But what his proposals for sectional reconciliation reveal is how irreconcilable the conflict had become. Crittenden and the Republicans started from diametrically opposed assumptions about the proper relationship between slavery and the federal government. Republican antislavery policies presupposed that slavery was strictly a state institution, that it had no claim to constitutional recognition beyond the borders of the states that legalized it. Every article of Crittenden's proposed amendment, and nearly all of his proposed congressional resolutions, rested on the opposite assumption—that slavery had powerful extraterritorial claims—claims beyond the borders of the states where it already existed. Crittenden believed he was offering the Republicans a meaningful compromise by proposing to restore the ban on slavery north of the Missouri Compromise line, but to Republicans the explicit federal recognition and protection of slavery in the southwestern territories, by means of a constitutional amendment no less, was a flagrant repudiation of the original Missouri settlement. When Republicans listened to Crittenden recite his resolutions they didn't hear a "compromise" proposal, they heard the terms of their own unconditional surrender.

But Republicans were no better able than Crittenden to formulate a viable compromise proposal that would settle

the gaping differences over slavery. They repeatedly disavowed any desire to overstep their constitutional obligation
to leave slavery alone in the states where it already existed. A
majority of Republicans were prepared to put that guarantee into the Constitution in the form of an amendment proposed by Ohio Republican Representative Thomas Corwin.
The "Corwin amendment" affirmed that under the Constitution Congress had no power "to abolish or interfere" with
the "domestic institutions" within any state. Many Republicans freely acknowledged that this was a superfluous ges-
ture. The slaveholders clearly understood that the Corwin
amendment would do nothing to protect slavery from the
scorpion's sting. Nor were any of the compromise proposals put forward by individual Republicans any more acceptable. Trumbull initially signaled his willingness to restore
the original terms of the Missouri Compromise, but then
backed away and like most Republicans called for a complete ban on slavery from all the territories. Twice Lincoln
offered a proposal to guarantee federal enforcement of the
fugitive-slave clause in exchange for due process rights of
accused fugitives—a proposal Seward warned him would
alienate their "friends" within the Republican Party—but
it hardly mattered because Lincoln's proposal fell on deaf
ears. Seward himself, for all his hopes of avoiding a war,
never put forward a single concrete proposal for sectional
compromise. Instead, he reiterated the same two choices
Republicans had been offering the slave states for years: a
peaceful program of gradual abolition within the Union, or
secession followed by the horrors of war and immediate, violent military emancipation.

Seward and his fellow Republican conciliators were no less sincere than Crittenden and his allies. From radicals like Thaddeus Stevens and Charles Sumner, from moderates like Abraham Lincoln and William Seward, from conservatives like John Sherman and Thomas Corwin—from every point on the Republican spectrum—came the same refrain: the Constitution does not allow the federal government to abolish slavery in the states where it already exists, and we have no intention of doing so. Every specific antislavery policy Republicans proposed was carefully designed to respect that constitutional restriction. Even the most radical of Radical Republicans promised to abide by the federal consensus. Indeed, it was precisely because they had been so careful to constrain themselves that Republicans had a hard time understanding what could possibly justify secession.

Benjamin Wade made this point when he temporarily broke the deliberate silence among Republicans in mid-December 1860. The prevailing "excitement" in the South was both "wild and unreasonable," Wade declared. "I have listened to the complaints on the other side patiently, and with an ardent desire to ascertain what was the particular difficulty under which they are laboring." But, he confessed, "I am totally unable to understand precisely what it is of which they complain."[21] Wade fully acknowledged that the Republicans were an antislavery party, that their platform precluded any compromise on the expansion of slavery in the territories. "I stand on that position to-day," he announced. It was well within the Constitution. But beyond the Constitution he vowed never to go. Indeed, "there is no Republican, there is no convention of Republicans, there is no paper that speaks for them, there is no orator that sets forth their doctrines, who ever pretends that they have any right in your States to interfere with your peculiar institution."[22]

And yet it's hard to imagine that any Southerner in Congress could have been mollified by anything Benjamin Wade said. Nobody was proposing federal abolition of slavery in the states; the Constitution already banned that, and Corwin's proposal merely reaffirmed the ban. Crittenden didn't even bother to include a version of the Corwin amendment in his own proposal because it removed a threat that did not exist. Instead, every one of Crittenden's proposed amendments would have restricted Washington's power over slavery in areas under *federal* rather than *state* control—the very areas where Republicans fully intended to attack slavery. For Crittenden and virtually all southern leaders, the only place where slavery needed stronger federal protection was in the free states, not the slave states.

Southern politicians certainly understood Republican intentions. In mid-January 1861, Missouri Congressman Trusten Polk denounced Republicans not for planning to abolish slavery in the states but for "their cherished object of surrounding the slaveholding States with a cordon of hostile non-slaveholding ones, and so either to smother the institution, or make it destroy itself; the scorpion, as they say, surrounded by fire."[23] Banning slavery from the territories was merely a means to this end, but in 1860 it was the most conspicuous and immediately threatening means by which Republicans hoped to set in motion the process of slavery's ultimate extinction. It was the policy that most frightened slavery's most ardent defenders. "*We must expand or perish,*" Robert Toombs explained. "We are constrained by an inexorable necessity to accept expansion or extermination." Southerners who denied this were fooling themselves, Toombs added. "The North understand it better—they have told us for twenty years that their object was to pen up slavery within its present limits—surround it with a border of free States, and like the scorpion surrounded by fire, they will make it sting itself to death."[24]

Secessionists were not fantasizing this doomsday scenario; they were simply repeating what Republicans themselves promised to do. It is hardly surprising, then, that secessionists were completely unmoved by ritualized Republican promises not to interfere with slavery in the states where it already existed. The "belief of the South," Louisiana Senator Judah P. Benjamin explained, is that "without intending to violate the letter of the Constitution by going into States for the purpose of forcibly emancipating slaves, it is the desire of the whole Republican party to close up the southern States with a cordon of free States for the avowed purpose of forcing the South the emancipate them."

Here was the nub of the secession crisis—at least according to Oregon's Republican Senator Edward Baker. The "great ground of complaint has now narrowed itself down to this," he declared in his reply to Judah Benjamin. "[W]e desire to circle the slave States with a cordon of free States, and thereby destroy the institution of slavery; to treat it like the scorpion girt by fire." Is this enough to justify secession, Baker asked the senator from Louisiana—is this adequate "ground of separation"?

"I say, yes," Benjamin shot back, "decidedly."[25]

⤞ 2 ⤝

The Right versus the
Wrong of Property in Man

W E'VE HEARD IT so often it's become a cliché: the Civil War was not about slavery, it was about the extension of slavery into the territories—a very different thing. Northerners wanted to preserve western settlement for free white men. They objected not to slavery itself but to the prospect of competing with slave laborers, or maybe they just wanted to keep black people out of the territories. The proof is everywhere you look. The so-called crisis of the 1850s was provoked not by some sudden outbreak of humanitarian sentiment in the North, but by the repeal of the Missouri Compromise that opened Kansas to slavery. The Dred Scott decision of 1857 was controversial not because the Supreme Court had justified slavery, but because the ruling made it impossible for Congress to block slavery's expansion. This was the crux of the famed Lincoln-Douglas debates the following year: Stephen A. Douglas would allow territorial settlers to have slavery if they wanted it, whereas Lincoln would preserve the territories for the benefit of free white settlers. He made this clear a few years later in his first inaugural address. I have no intention, Lincoln said, of interfering with slavery in the states where it already exists. The issue was not slavery itself, it was the expansion of slavery into the territories.

But we've already seen that denials of the sort Lincoln made were pro forma even among the most radical Republicans. Charles Sumner, Benjamin Wade, Salmon P. Chase, Thaddeus Stevens—all of them disavowed any intention of interfering with slavery in the states where it already existed, yet all of them just as firmly avowed their hatred of slavery and their determination to use whatever constitutional power Congress had to destroy it, however long that might take. The point of the scorpion's sting was to surround slavery until it killed itself, and crucial to that project was banning slavery from the territories. Viewed in this light, the familiar cliché might easily be reversed: the Civil War was only superficially a dispute over slavery in the territories; in reality it was a fundamental conflict over slavery.

IF THIS DOES NOT seem obvious to us, it may be because it is no longer obvious to us what slavery was and, therefore, what a dispute over slavery would look like. This is not because slavery means so little to Americans, but because it has come to mean too much. Slavery has long served as the rhetorical standard against which all forms of oppression are measured. Among men and women who struggle against various forms of their own oppression, there seems to be a nearly irresistible temptation to liken themselves to slaves. In the United States this urge was validated in the very Revolution that brought the nation into being. The colonists fighting for independence from Great Britain commonly equated their condition with slavery. "*Those* who are *taxed* without their own consent," John Dickinson wrote, "are *slaves. We are taxed* without our consent expressed by ourselves or our representatives. *We* are therefore—SLAVES."[1] Even before the War of Independence the opprobrium associated with slavery splattered onto other forms of inequity. American colonists inhabited a world in which owning land was the key to independence and those without it were sometimes described as slaves. "They who have no property can have no freedom," Stephen Hopkins explained in 1765, "but are indeed reduced to the most abject slavery."[2] Nineteenth-century feminists made a similar point about patriarchy. "The wife who inherits no property," Elizabeth Cady Stanton wrote in 1854, "holds about the same legal position than does the slave on the southern plantation."[3] Early labor agitators sometimes denounced the evils of "wage slavery." Frederick Douglass once said that whereas blacks in the South were enslaved to individual masters, blacks in the North were slaves to their communities. Carl Schurz said nearly the same thing about white Southerners. "[B]y the necessities arising from their condition," Schurz argued in 1860, ordinary southern whites were "the slaves of slavery."[4] The analogy was everywhere during the sectional crisis. As early as 1837 John C. Calhoun declared that white Southerners had to resist the "aggression" of antislavery Northerners, or be "prepared to be slaves themselves."[5] Secessionists said the same thing decades later: we must leave the Union or be enslaved to the abolitionists.

Collapsing the distinction between slavery and other forms of inequality poses special problems for anyone trying to figure out the origins of the Civil War because if everything was slavery, what can it possibly mean to say that slavery caused the Civil War? If poor southern whites were the slaves of wealthy planters, if northern and southern wives were alike enslaved to their husbands, if wage earners were slaves to their employers and free blacks slaves of their communities—if even slaveholders felt enslaved to their putative northern masters—if slavery was everywhere in mid-nineteenth-century America, it was nowhere in particular. Hence the problem: if you cannot specify what slavery was, you won't know what a conflict over slavery looked like.

Part of the problem is that many of slavery's most degrading features—physical cruelty, debased status, forced labor, and sexual exploitation—were not unique to slavery. This makes it easy to lump different forms of subordination together, to throw up our hands in frustration and decry the fact that throughout human history the mass of men and women have led lives of quiet desperation. But that doesn't help us understand what slavery was. Another problem is slavery's remarkable adaptability. Slaves have worked in mines, on plantations, in schools, in harems, in armies and navies. There have been rural slaves and urban slaves. Slaves sometimes owned other slaves. Some slaves have enjoyed high status, some were miserable but well fed, others were worked to death. Slavery has flourished in so many different times and places, it has served so many different purposes, as to defy succinct description. Yet if we are to use a single word—*slavery*—to describe such a variety of situations over so vast a span of centuries, we ought to be especially careful to specify just what that word means.[6]

Historians have not always been helpful in this regard. Too often they have succumbed to the temptation to relativize slavery, to define it in ways that obscure its distinctive attributes. One influential strand of scholarship erases the distinction between slavery and kinship, subsuming various forms of "unfreedom" under the general heading of "patriarchy." Another influential interpretation, deriving from the fact that New World slavery was eventually restricted to sub-Saharan Africans and their descendants, defines slavery as an extreme form of racial discrimination. We come closer to the main issue when we turn our attention to the nature of slave labor, but not close enough. No one disputes that slavery was "at bottom" a labor system, but so was feudalism, so was the family farm, and so for that matter is capitalism. They're all, at bottom, labor systems.

Eventually this relativizing tendency, this urge to equate slavery with very different forms of inequality—in particular with patriarchy—prompted some of the best scholars in the field to begin sending up warning flares. David Brion Davis was one of the first to caution against overly broad categories. "The concept of chattel slavery," he insisted, "must be distinguished from historical varieties of servitude and dependence." M. I. Finley went further a few years later. "That all forms of involuntary labour can be classed in a single category is self-evident," Finley explained in 1980. "But is that a useful classification?" Are there not "self-evident differences among the various kinds of compulsory labor?" Finley was particularly concerned to distinguish slave labor from "the work of women and children within the family, no matter how authoritarian and patriarchal its structure." Like Davis, Finley located the distinctive characteristic of slavery in the "chattel principle." "As a commodity," he wrote, "the slave is property." Claude Meillasoux was no less emphatic. Resisting what he saw as "the assimilation of slavery to kinship" in African studies, Meillasoux bluntly declared that "in fact the two are strictly antinomic." Slaves were commodities in ways that wives and children never were. In the final analysis, Meillasoux argued, "the real or potential fate of the slaves—their *state* in other words—is necessarily defined with respect to the market." For these scholars the "chattel principle" was crucial—slaves were commodified property. This more than anything distinguished slavery from other forms of inequality.[7]

The North and South did not go to war because they disagreed about patriarchy. Nor was the Civil War sparked by a disagreement over racial discrimination. Patriarchy and racial discrimination existed in both sections and they did not cause any substantial disagreement. What tore the nation apart was a dispute over two very different labor systems, and the crucial difference between them was, once again, the chattel principle. Here was the issue debated everywhere during the sectional crisis. To fight over slavery was to disagree about the moral, political, economic, and constitutional legitimacy of what Americans at the time called "property in man."

More importantly, the specific questions about slavery that roiled American public life in the middle of the nineteenth century—Should slavery be excluded from the territories?

Could Congress abolish it in the District of Columbia? Who should enforce the fugitive-slave clause?—arose only because supporters and opponents of slavery had diametrically opposed answers to a more fundamental question: did the natural right of property take precedence over the natural right to freedom?

Slaveholders answered that question by pointing out that the nation was founded, to a very large degree, to defend the inalienable right of property. It was a standard precept of Anglo-American political philosophy that the protection of property was a primary reason—arguably *the* primary reason—for establishing *any* form of government. Not surprisingly, the Constitution prohibited Congress from depriving anyone of property without due process of law. This was not an absolute right—governments in early America often took property *with* the due process of law— nor did the Constitution specifically protect *slave* property. Nevertheless, slaveholders had no doubt that a right of "property in man" was sanctioned by the Constitution, even if it did not explicitly say so. "There was an implied contract between the Northern and Southern people," Congressman William Smith of South Carolina explained in the 1790s, "that no step should be taken to injure the property of the latter."[8]

In saying that the protection of slave property was "implied," Smith was not surreptitiously smuggling a defense of slavery into the Constitution. Instead, he was assuming that the Constitution was written to defend a right of property that already existed under the laws of nature. Long before there was a Constitution there was a natural right of property that was "higher" than constitutional law.

"[T]he right of property preceded the constitution," a Southern State Convention in Mississippi declared in 1849. "[I]t is coeval with the history of man; it exists by a paramount law of nature." The Kentucky legislature said the same thing. The right of property "is before and higher than any constitutional sanction."[9] This same "higher law" principle was enshrined in the controversial Lecompton Constitution of 1857, which would have legalized slavery in Kansas. "The right of property is before and higher than any constitutional sanction," it declared, "and the right of the owner of a slave to such and its increase is the same, and as inviolable, as the right of the owner of any property whatsoever."[10] Thus slavery itself was sanctioned by principles of natural right that transcended mere statutes. As late as 1864 northern Democrats were still claiming that slavery "is not the creature of law." On the contrary, New York Congressman Fernando Wood declared, slavery "existed without law before this Government was established."[11]

When slavery's defenders invoked "higher law," they were not rejecting the Constitution or even stepping beyond it. On the contrary, most Americans who gave the matter any serious thought believed that the precepts of "higher law" were embedded within the Constitution—that the Constitution itself was in part a natural law document. Higher, or natural, law was not extraconstitutional law. At the very least this meant that the right of property in slaves was implicit in the Constitution. The natural right of property in man was, by this reasoning, a constitutional right, even though not expressly written down in the 1787 document.

The idea that slavery could exist "without law," even before any government was established, helps explain some of the difficulty historians have had in tracing the origins of slavery in the seventeenth-century Chesapeake. When the first British colonies were founded in North America, settlers simply assumed that slavery was secure. Because slaves were property, no special slave code—no "positive law"—was needed, because the rights of property were already recognized and protected in the original charters establishing the colonies themselves. English settlers at Jamestown had no trouble accepting that those first nineteen blacks who landed in 1620 were already slaves. They had been purchased in Africa as slaves and brought to America by means of an already elaborate and well-established transatlantic slave trade. This does not mean that the precise terms of their enslavement were settled from the start. As in many slave societies, a number of the earliest slaves in the Chesapeake were later manumitted. Yet from the very beginning Africans were sold to the Virginians as slave property, and within a year or two slave property was showing up in the wills of colonial settlers who were already bequeathing it to specific heirs. Historians searching for the origins of Chesapeake slavery in a statute that formally created slavery have been universally thwarted. Except for Massachusetts and Georgia, which had to overturn a ban on slavery, no other colonies ever passed a law that simply established slavery, because no such laws were thought to be needed. Slaves were by definition property, and property was already protected—if not by positive law in the form of a colonial charter, or by common law, then by "higher law," natural law. For the most part, statutes were necessary to abolish slavery, not to create it.[12]

Yet even as North American slavery was developing on these assumptions in the seventeenth century, the English Civil War was generating a radical impulse that would overturn the premise that slavery was protected as part of the natural right of property prior to the formation of governments. The natural condition of human beings was freedom, English radicals like "freeborn" John Lilburne and Algernon Sidney declared. The original right of property derived from a prior and even more fundamental natural right of self-ownership—the primary claim that all people owned, if nothing else, themselves. By extension, self-ownership included a proprietary claim to your own labor and with it the fruits of your own labor. That's where all property came from, hence the right of property itself originated in the universal, natural right of freedom—freedom defined as self-ownership. "The property which every man has in his own labour," Adam Smith wrote, "as it is the original foundation of all other property, so it is the most sacred and inviolable."[13] This made freedom the first of all the natural rights—the inalienable right from which all "alienable" forms of property derived. By this reasoning freedom, not slavery, was the normal condition of every human being. Only positive laws could overrule this presumption of freedom.

In the late seventeenth century English judges began to apply this revolutionary doctrine to slavery. Freedom, they increasingly ruled, was the default condition of everyone on English soil, and that presumed condition of freedom could only be overridden by a "positive" law explicitly establishing slavery. Not until 1772, however, did this doctrine become a permanent feature of English law. In that year Lord Mansfield, the chief justice of the Court of King's Bench, issued his famous ruling in the case known as *Somerset*. There was no natural or common-law right of property in man, Mansfield ruled. On the contrary, slavery was so complete a violation of the natural right to freedom that only "positive" law could *create* slavery. Such laws existed in Britain's colonies, but not in England itself. Thus, the moment slaves set foot on English soil the property claims of their masters vanished and slavery itself became one of those run-of-the-mill servile statuses—apprenticeship or indenture, for example—with which Englishmen were familiar. Slaves were no longer commodities; they were merely "persons held to service." This was the *Somerset* principle—at least as it was widely interpreted in the northern colonies and, later, states.

Here was another "higher law," different from the one invoked by slaveholders during the sectional crisis. What the Founders had actually embedded in the Constitution, slavery's opponents believed, was not the natural right of property in man but the "higher law" of universal freedom. Didn't the preamble to the Constitution promise to "secure the blessings of liberty" to "we, the people" of the United States, "to ourselves and our Posterity"? Hadn't the men who drafted the Constitution deliberately refused to recognize slaves as property? Was it merely an accident that the fugitive-slave and three-fifths clauses of the Constitution referred not to property but to "persons held to service"?

By the late 1830s this revolutionary "freedom principle" had emerged as the philosophical rationale for an increasingly aggressive antislavery politics. Reversing proslavery premises, antislavery writers, lawyers, and politicians insisted that what preceded government was not the natural right of property, but the natural right of *freedom*. This was the doctrine William Seward declared in his famous "higher law" speech during the ferocious debates over the Compromise of 1850. For Republicans freedom was the natural, default condition, the presumed status of everyone living under the protection of the Constitution, unless expressly overruled by a positive law enacted by a sovereign state. The doctrine was enshrined in the Republican Party's 1860 platform resolution quoted in chapter one, the resolution declaring that "the normal condition of all the territory of the United States is that of freedom."

By the 1850s, then, the debate over slavery was framed around two competing principles of "higher law." Proslavery constitutionalism started from the assumption that slaves were property and as such were subsumed under the natural rights of property. This right was embedded in the Constitution, whether implicitly, as South Carolina's William Smith had argued, or "expressly," as Chief Justice Roger Taney claimed in the Dred Scott decision of 1857. Antislavery constitutionalism started from the opposite premise, that the natural right of freedom preceded government but was enshrined in the Constitution itself, that slaves were property only in states whose positive laws overrode the presumption of freedom. Or, as Abraham Lincoln put it at Cooper Union in February 1860, there was no such thing as a constitutional right of property in slaves.

NONE OF THIS is to suggest that the Civil War was caused by a philosophical disagreement about the relationship between slavery and natural law. The causes of the war are many and complicated. Even the most fundamental philosophical differences can be smoothed over by policy compromises that neither side likes but enough people are willing to accept. But that there *was* a fundamental philosophical disagreement over slavery, over both the moral and legal status of property in man, is clear enough. In every major dispute over the appropriate relationship between slavery and the federal government, the debate was framed in these broader philosophical terms. This was true of the fugitive-slave controversy that erupted in the 1850s, and it was equally true of the conflict over slavery in the territories that broke out in the 1840s. But the first place it appeared was during the debate over the abolition of slavery in Washington, D.C., beginning in the 1830s.

On the surface it's not clear why proposals to abolish slavery in the District of Columbia should have raised any constitutional objections. Article I, Section 8, gives Congress the power of "exclusive legislation" over the District, "in all cases whatsoever." That would seem to settle the question of whether the federal government could abolish slavery in Washington. District abolition might be imprudent, but upon what *legal* grounds could anyone object to it? The proslavery answer was: slavery is protected by the Constitution as an inalienable right of property, and under the Fifth Amendment the Congress has no power to take away that right. The antislavery response was: the due process clause of the Fifth Amendment, far from recognizing a constitutional right to property in human beings, in fact assumes universal freedom.

The issue arose as early as 1827, when the House committee governing the District asserted that in Washington, D.C., as in the slaveholding states, all blacks were *presumed* to be slaves unless they could prove their freedom. Free blacks who were mistakenly arrested as runaways were required to pay all the legal fees arising from their arrest, and anyone who could not pay was "liable to be sold into slavery." As Massachusetts Senator Henry Wilson later explained, "every colored man whose feet pressed the soil of the District was presumed to be a slave." Here was an early version of the question raised by the struggle to abolish slavery in Washington: in areas over which the federal government was sovereign, did the Constitution presume slavery, or did it presume freedom?[14]

That issue came to a head on January 6, 1829, when Pennsylvania Congressman Charles Miner introduced a series of resolutions in the House decrying the nefarious operations of the domestic slave trade in the nation's capital and denouncing the federal government for its role in "carrying on this traffic in human beings." Like earlier generations of abolitionists in England and America, Miner believed that the abolition of the slave trade in the District was a first step toward complete abolition. His resolution asked for a congressional investigation into a number of allegations—that District prisons were used as holding pens for slaves sold in the domestic trade, that free blacks were subject to arbitrary arrest and enslavement, that families were cruelly broken apart. Miner also asked that a congressional committee be "instructed to inquire into the expediency of providing by law for the gradual abolition of slavery within the District."[15]

In defense of his resolutions, Miner complained about the effect the "presumption" of slavery had on free blacks. "It seems to me a hardship," he said, "that persons born free in New York, Pennsylvania, or elsewhere, who perhaps never thought of a certificate of freedom, should, without any charge of crime, if they come within this District, be thrown into prison." He thought the burden of proof should be on the slave traders. They should be required to present evidence that their victims were legally enslaved *before* "raising a presumption that they are runaway slaves, before they should be deprived of personal liberty." Along the way Miner laced his argument with denunciations of the brutality of slavery and its violation of both republican principles and Christian values.[16]

Maryland Congressman John Weems replied immediately, disputing Miner's facts, bridling at the accusations of unchristian behavior, denouncing the Pennsylvania congressman for "meddling" in other people's business and for violating the principle of church/state separation by attempting to use the law to impose his private religious convictions on people who did not share them. But mostly Weems demanded that Northerners like Miner "discontinue their unrighteous interference with the right . . . we hold in this species of property." What made Miner's interference "unrighteous," as opposed to merely illegal, was that it violated the scriptural sanction for slavery evident throughout the Bible—which Weems proceeded to quote at length (even though, only minutes earlier, he had denounced antislavery congressmen for attempting to impose their own religious views on Southerners). Of all the "higher law" arguments put forward in defense of slavery, this was the most popular: the right of property in man, though recognized by the Constitution, originated in the law of God.[17]

Miner's antislavery resolutions went nowhere, buried in a committee stacked with proslavery representatives. This only stoked the determination of abolitionists, and by the mid-1830s they launched a massive petition campaign against slavery and the slave trade in Washington, D.C. At first, northern representatives like former president John Quincy Adams politely accepted the petitions, but dismissed the significance of abolition in the District of Columbia. But when proslavery representatives tried to "gag" the antislavery petitions, they provoked a heated response on the floor of Congress and beyond.

Proslavery congressmen justified the gag rule on the ground that in demanding District abolition the petitioners were asking Congress to pass a law that was unconstitutional—a law that would violate the slaveholders' rights of property. "I think the House should not receive the petition," Congressman James Henry Hammond of South Carolina argued, "because it asks us to do what we have no constitutional power to do." The Constitution, he added, "recognizes slaves as *property*" and forbids the government from taking private property except for "public purposes," and even then it guarantees the property owner "just compensation." Hammond did not deny that the Constitution granted Congress the exclusive power to legislate for the

District, but, he wondered, "how far that power will, of itself, extend?" The purpose of all legislation, Hammond went on, is "to *protect* life, liberty, and *property*." He added a classic recitation of the principle of negative liberty: "If the slave owner is deprived of the full use of his property, unless that use impairs the rights of others, you can as well deprive him of the property itself."[18] The master's exercise of his property rights was limited only at the point where the exercise impinged on the property rights of others. For Hammond depriving *slaves* of their freedom did not impinge on their rights because, of course, slaves were property and therefore had no rights.

Once the supporters of slavery in the District raised the issue of property rights, it was no longer enough for the opponents of slavery to note that the Constitution gave Congress exclusive authority to legislate for the District. For if slaves were constitutionally protected property, the power to legislate—even the *exclusive* power—could not reasonably entail the power to deprive citizens of their constitutionally protected property. In their efforts to justify the abolition of slavery in Washington, D.C., abolitionists were thereby forced to confront a fundamental question: did the Constitution protect slavery as a right of property?

In 1838 the abolitionist Theodore Dwight Weld answered the property-rights argument in his influential pamphlet, *The Power of Congress over Slavery in the District of Columbia*. He began with the higher-law premise that every human being is endowed with the natural right of freedom. This freedom principle, Weld argued, was put into the Constitution by a generation of Founders who not only hated slavery but who assumed that over time "the moral sense of the nation," acting through legislatures, schools, and abolition societies, would create "a power of opinion that would abolish the system throughout the nation." The Founders' abhorrence of slavery, Weld said, was expressed in the language of the Constitution recognizing slaves only as "persons," never as "property." There could be no constitutional right of property in slaves, Weld went on, because, as everyone knew, the right of property originated in self-ownership. By the consent of the entire civilized world "slaves are not '*property*,' but *self-proprietors*." To own a slave as property was not a natural but merely a legal right, created "only by *positive legislative acts*, forcibly setting aside the law of nature, the common law, and the principles of universal justice and right between man and man." Beyond the limits of the slave states, wherever the Constitution was sovereign, the right of self-ownership prevailed. In vesting Congress with sovereignty over Washington, D.C., then, the Constitution necessarily granted the federal government the power to abolish slavery in the nation's capital.[19]

Several distinct questions arose in the decades-long debate over the abolition of slavery in Washington, D.C. Some were pragmatic: even if Congress had the power to abolish slavery, was it wise to do so? Some were legalistic: what specific powers did the Constitution refer to when it vested Congress with "exclusive" legislative authority over the District? Yet for a quarter of a century, from the late 1830s until Congress finally abolished slavery in Washington, D.C., in 1862, the terms of the debate never really changed. The situation was in many ways sui generis. There was no other place quite like the District of Columbia. Yet the issues raised by the abolition of slavery in Washington, D.C., were broad and general. At stake was the legitimacy of slavery itself, the right versus the wrong of "property in man."

THE SAME WAS TRUE of the fugitive-slave controversy. Once again a number of distinct issues arose: the relative power of state versus federal government, the constitutional limits of interstate comity—that is, how far any state had to go to respect the laws of other states—and not least the question of who was responsible for the enforcement of the fugitive-slave clause of the Constitution. But none of these issues could have provoked much controversy had there not been an underlying disagreement over slavery itself, over the moral and constitutional legitimacy of "property in man." From the late 1830s onward, just about every dispute over fugitive-slave rendition turned on the question of whether a free state was obliged to respect the laws of slave states that treated fugitives as "property."

Often the issue arose when Northerners who assisted runaway slaves were charged with "theft." In one of the earliest incidents of this nature—in May 1837—the governor of Maine refused to extradite the captain of a ship on which a Georgia slave had stowed away. When the ship docked in Maine the slave came ashore and escaped to Canada. The governor of Georgia pronounced the captain a fugitive from justice who should be sent south and charged with slave stealing. But Maine's governor refused the extradition request on the ground that in his state slaves were considered persons rather than property. Property could be stolen, but not persons. Hence the captain had committed no crime recognized by the laws of Maine.[20]

Two years later it happened again, in a much more widely publicized case, pitting the state of New York against the state of Virginia. In July 1839, one of John Colby's slaves, a man named Isaac, stowed away on board a schooner out of Norfolk. This time the escape attempt failed. Upon reaching New York the slave was seized and returned to Virginia. Not satisfied with the successful rendition of the slave, however, Virginia's governor demanded that the captain of the schooner be extradited and put on trial for violating Virginia's law against slave stealing. The tit-for-tat began. New York's governor, William Seward, refused to extradite the captain for something that was not a crime under New York law. Next the New York legislature passed an antikidnapping statute, guaranteeing all accused fugitives a right to trial by jury. The Virginia legislature responded in turn with a resolution declaring that "the stealing of a slave within the jurisdiction of Virginia was a crime within the meaning of the Constitution." This suggested that owning slaves was constitutionally protected as a right of property and that New York was therefore obliged to adhere to the Virginia law outlawing the theft of slave property. New York was under no such obligation, Governor Seward replied. And why not? Because, he said, "beings possessed of the physical, moral, and intellectual faculties common to the human race, cannot, by the force of any constitution or laws, be goods or chattels, or a thing." He would not enforce Virginia's law against slave stealing because in the state of New York only "goods, chattels, and things can be the subject of larceny, stealing, or theft."[21] The crimes reveal the conflicting premises about persons and property: when Northerners assisted in the escape of slaves, the southern states charged them with "theft." When Southerners went into the North to capture fugitives, the northern states charged them with "kidnapping."

The same conflict over the status of slave "property" reappeared in all of the major fugitive-slave cases that made their way through the state and federal courts in the two or three decades before the Civil War—the Prigg case, the Van Zandt case, the Aves case, the Latimer case, and, of course, the Dred Scott case. The opponents of slavery consistently argued that the free states were under no obligation to enforce the fugitive-slave clause of the Constitution because slave property had no legal standing in the North. Slaves were property only under the laws of the states that made them property, Salmon P. Chase explained. Like Theodore Dwight Weld, Chase dismissed property in slaves as a "naked legal" right, by which he meant a right that existed only where a state statute created it. But there was no natural right to slave property, Chase insisted, nor was there a constitutional right—for the Constitution clearly referred to slaves only as "persons," never as property. Whenever a slave escaped into a free state, the master's legal claim on the slave as property vanished, and the slave became, under both Ohio law and under the Constitution, a "person held to service."

Chase lost that case. So did every abolitionist lawyer who argued, before the Supreme Court, that because slavery was strictly a state institution the fugitive-slave clause should be enforced in the northern states only as those states saw fit. Stacked with proslavery Democrats, the Supreme Court repeatedly rejected the antislavery reading of the Constitution. From Prigg to Dred Scott, the justices insisted with increasing vehemence that slaves were property, not persons, under the Constitution. Along the way the defense of slave property became increasingly aggressive. Back in the 1830s many southern Whigs accepted that property rights were not absolute, that not all property was the same, and that it was a normal and necessary function of government to put limits on property rights. At that point only a handful of Southerners—John C. Calhoun and Jefferson Davis among them—argued that property rights were absolute and indivisible. By the 1850s they were no longer in the minority.

This more radical proslavery position consisted of three distinct elements. First, the rights of property were virtually absolute; government had no business interfering with or regulating property beyond what was necessary to ensure that everyone's rights were equally protected. Second, as far as the Constitution was concerned, all property was identical—there was no legal distinction between a house, a cow, a chair, or a slave—all were protected as property in exactly the same way. Third, wherever the Constitution was sovereign—on the high seas, in the territories, in Washington, D.C.—the federal government was obliged to protect the right of property in slaves if for any reason local authorities failed to do so.

BY THE 1850s, when the territorial issue roiled national politics, supporters and opponents of slavery brought to

the table two radicalized and antithetical views of the constitutional status of "property in man." As with the question
of whether Congress had the power to abolish slavery in
Washington, or the status of fugitive slaves on free soil, the
territorial question—far from being an evasion of the main
issue—was in fact another occasion for addressing it.

That slavery's expansion was the most persistent and
contentious of those occasions, no serious historian disputes. It kept coming up. In the 1790s opponents of slavery
were already trying to exclude slavery from the southwestern territories. It came up in Missouri in 1820, in Arkansas
and Florida in the 1830s, in Texas in the 1840s, in Kansas
in the 1850s, in Arizona and New Mexico during the secession crisis. This is hardly surprising, given how much was
at stake in the territorial question. Even if Congress had
abolished slavery in Washington, D.C., in 1840, even if the
opponents of slavery had successfully restricted enforcement of the fugitive-slave clause to the states in 1850—the
effects on slavery in the South would have been negligible.
Not so with slavery in the territories. The political power
of the slave states and the economic prospects for slavery
itself had always depended heavily on its ability to expand
into the western territories—into Louisiana, into Alabama
and Mississippi, into Texas, and, if unchecked, into the
mining districts of the mountain states, southward into
Central America, and beyond the Florida keys into Cuba
and who knows where else. With each new acquisition, the
power of the slave states in the federal government was bol-
stered anew and the economic life of slavery was extended.
For slavery's defenders, expansion was a matter of life and

death. For slavery's opponents, halting its expansion was the line in the sand.

In 1848 John C. Calhoun asked, "Has the North the power" to keep slavery out of the territories? Not under the Constitution, he answered. Indeed, slavery was "the only property recognized" by the Constitution. If anything, the fact that "the South holds property in slaves" created what Calhoun called "a strong presumption against" the power to restrict slavery's expansion. There's that word again—*presumption*—and it figured prominently in Calhoun's argument. The Constitution established a "presumption" in favor of the rights of slaveholders to bring their property into federal territories, and the northern states had no power to override that presumption.[22] The Dred Scott decision reaffirmed Calhoun's radicalized proslavery position. The Constitution, Chief Justice Taney insisted, "expressly" recognized a right of property in slaves; it treated slave property in exactly the same way it treated every other form of property—thus shielding slavery under the protective cover of a near-absolute right of property.

This was the argument that Abraham Lincoln, and virtually all Republicans, contested ever more strenuously over the course of the 1850s. One-sixth of our population are slaves, Lincoln noted in 1860. "The owners of these slaves consider them property. The effect upon the minds of the owners is that of property, and nothing else—it induces them to insist upon all that will favorably affect its value as property, to demand laws and institutions and a public policy that shall increase and secure its value." Unlike slaveholders, Lincoln argued, Northerners could not see slavery through the "medium" of property. They argued from a very different presumption. "To us," Lincoln explained, "it appears natural to think that slaves are human beings; *men*, not property." Slavery's defenders had no trouble accepting that a human being could be property. They never thought they were treating their slaves as anything other than human beings. Property, after all, came in many different varieties. Some property was animate (horses), some was inanimate (a piano); some was "real" (land); some was abstract (a dollar bill); and some property, specifically slave property, was human. But for slavery's opponents the concept of "human property" was a self-contradiction. Thus, for Lincoln, you could either treat people like property or you could treat them like human beings, but you could not do both. As always with Lincoln, it was not the uniqueness of his position that stands out, but the clarity with which he expressed it.

Like nearly all Republicans, Lincoln believed that the conflict over slavery was, at bottom, a fundamental disagreement over property rights in human beings. "Now these two ideas, the property idea that Slavery is right, and the idea that it is wrong, come into collision," Lincoln concluded, and could not help but produce two very different federal policies. "The first, based on the property view that Slavery is right, conforms to that idea throughout, and demands that we shall do everything for it that we ought to do if it were right. . . . The other policy is one that squares with the idea that Slavery is wrong, and it consists in doing everything that we ought to do if it is wrong."[23]

THE RIGHT VERSUS the wrong of "property in man"—that's what a fundamental conflict over slavery most often came down to. If slaves were a constitutionally protected species of property, Congress could not legitimately abolish slavery in the nation's capital, the northern states could not legitimately interfere with the capture and return of fugitive slaves, and the federal government could not discriminate against southern migrants by excluding their slave property from the "common" territories of the United States. But if slavery was purely a state institution, if under the Constitution slaves were recognized not as property but as "persons held to service," the individual states were free to regulate fugitive-slave rendition as they saw fit and the federal government was within its rights to free the slaves in the nation's capital. If there was no such thing as a constitutional right of property in slaves, Congress could ban slavery from the western territories. If by late 1860 a civil war was not inevitable, if armed conflict was to be averted, if enough secessionists and enough Republicans were willing to compromise, the issue they would have to compromise was the right of property in human beings.

But not all human beings. Nobody was claiming property rights in white people. When proslavery writers and politicians defended the right of property in man, they meant *black* men. For New World slavery was *racial* slavery, and that made it impossible to debate about slavery without also debating about race.

✥ 3 ✥

Race Conflict

H AVING NARROWLY DEFEATED Abraham Lincoln and
won reelection to the U.S. Senate in 1858, Stephen
A. Douglas decided to return to Washington from Illinois by
the southern route, stopping along the way to give a series
of speeches in the Mississippi River towns of Memphis, Saint
Louis, and New Orleans. Commenting on the recent campaign, Douglas explained how his own position on the great
issue of the day differed from Lincoln's. He reiterated his
conviction that slavery would expand only into territories
where it was suited by climate and geography. In some places
voters would legalize slavery and in others they would reject
it, depending on whether it was adaptable by nature to that
particular area. Such were the iron laws linking politics with
geography, Douglas claimed, that not even an abolitionist
could repeal them. Should antislavery Congressman Joshua
Giddings, for example, be somehow transferred from Ohio
to Louisiana, he would inevitably become "an advocate of

slavery" and would, Douglas predicted, "materially modify his opinions on negro equality." Once in the South, Giddings would see "that it was a question between the negro and the crocodile, and not between the white man and the negro." In any contest between "the white man and the negro," Douglas would side with the white man. But in any contest between "the negro and the crocodile," Douglas joked, he would stand shoulder to shoulder "for the negro against the crocodile."[1]

Quoting Douglas's remarks a little over a year later in New Haven, Connecticut, Abraham Lincoln unleashed a furious counterattack. Senator Douglas's true meaning "is just this," Lincoln explained. "As a white man is to a negro, so is a negro to a crocodile; and as the negro may rightfully treat the crocodile, so may the white man rightfully treat the negro." By using language like that, Lincoln complained, Douglas was trying to "brutalize the negro," and in so doing "to bring public opinion to the point of utter indifference whether men so brutalized are enslaved or not." The senator's remarks were not only crude, Lincoln insisted, they were also fallacious. Douglas was assuming that "there is a struggle between the white man and the negro in which either the white man must enslave the negro or the negro must enslave the white man. There is no such struggle!" Lincoln declared. "It is merely an ingenious falsehood, to degrade and brutalize the negro. Let each let the other alone, and there is no struggle about it. . . . This good earth is plenty broad enough for white man and negro both." According to the newspaper reports of the speech, Lincoln's audience interrupted him with "continued applause."[2]

IT WAS IMPOSSIBLE for Stephen Douglas and Abraham Lincoln to argue about slavery without also arguing about race, and what was true of the two Illinois politicians was true for millions of Americans. To be sure, within the slave states where there was little disagreement over slavery, there was consequently little debate over race beyond the question of whether blacks were created as a separate species or an innately inferior category of human beings. But between antislavery Northerners and proslavery Southerners, and between northern Democrats and northern Republicans, the debate over slavery spilled over into a corresponding debate over racial equality and inequality in the United States.

As the decades passed and the conflict over slavery became more heated, the dispute over racial equality settled on a handful of straightforward questions. For example, were blacks and whites equally entitled to the fruits of their labor? Among antislavery politicians like Abraham Lincoln the answer was, unambiguously, yes. In the right to the bread she earns from the sweat of her brow, Lincoln often said, the black woman is my equal, and Stephen A. Douglas's equal, and the equal of any living man. But for a proslavery author like Edmund Ruffin, the answer was no, because blacks were racially immune to the motivating force of wage labor; they would not work except by compulsion.

Americans disagreed on several other issues of racial equality in the middle decades of the nineteenth century, but two questions were widely debated and genuinely explosive. The first and most important of these questions was:

Does the promise of universal freedom in the Declaration
of Independence apply to whites and blacks alike?

Republicans said yes, northern Democrats and most
white Southerners said no. From this broad disagreement
on fundamental principles arose a second, explosive question, one that had been simmering for some time but did
not become central until the Dred Scott decision of 1857:

Were blacks citizens?

Although these two questions clearly grew out of the
debate over slavery, strictly speaking both were about specific forms of racial equality. Indeed, the citizenship question
could only arise in relation to *free* blacks because, except for
a handful of the most radical abolitionists, nearly everyone
agreed that slaves were not citizens by definition.

It's no surprise that the issues of race and slavery were
so closely related. New World slavery was, after all, *racial*
slavery. The condition of slavery—being owned as chattel—
was reserved exclusively for people defined as "racially" distinct. Initially this may have included Native Americans, but
eventually only blacks were enslaved on the basis of their
supposed racial identity. To justify slavery, then, it was not
enough to defend the sanctity of property rights, you also
had to explain why only black people should be treated as
property. This created some problems for proslavery writers, particularly proslavery theologians. As staunch biblical
literalists, they had no trouble finding scriptural support for
slavery, in both the Old and the New Testament. But they

scoured the pages of the Bible in vain, always coming away empty-handed, whenever they tried to find scriptural sanction for the specific enslavement of black people. Abandoning their own literalism, proslavery theologians retreated to obscure hermeneutics, mistranslations, and imaginative readings of ambiguous passages in their determined efforts to limit property in man to Africans and their descendants.

In theory, the argument against slavery was easier because it required only a single step. Once you rejected the legitimacy of property rights in human beings, you were done. There was no need to talk about race at all, and indeed one of the most distinctive things about Republicans was their tendency to avoid the subject of race. What Eric Foner has said about Lincoln can be extended to Republicans in general: race is our obsession, it was not theirs. Yet if they were not obsessed with race, neither could Republicans avoid it. Overwhelmed by a lava flow of racial demagoguery spewing forth from Democrats across the North, Lincoln and the Republicans often had no choice but to confront the issue of racial equality.

None of this means that Republicans in the 1850s and 1860s spoke for an enlightened northern electorate that advocated racial equality as Americans have come to understand it in the decades since the civil rights movement. We know they did not. Northern blacks in Lincoln's day were free, but they were not equal. They enjoyed many of the ordinary rights and privileges of free people, but they were also discriminated against in any number of ways. Unlike slaves, northern blacks were entitled to legally secure families, but marriage between blacks and whites was usually illegal. Free blacks were entitled to the fruits of their labor, but they were excluded from skilled jobs and paid less for doing the same work whites performed. When accused of a crime or bringing a lawsuit, free blacks in the North were entitled to the rights of due process—trial by jury and habeas corpus, for example—but for the most part only whites could serve on juries. Northern blacks were citizens, but as with women and children, citizenship did not entail the right to vote or hold public office. Some northern blacks could vote, but most could not. Segregation was widespread—blacks were separated from whites in public schools, railways, and streetcars, as well as in privately owned theaters, restaurants, hotels, and even cemeteries. There were significant limits to how far racial egalitarianism went in the northern states, even among many of the most vocal opponents of slavery.

Republicans talked about race less in terms of "equality" than in terms of differential "rights." There was something close to consensus among Republicans that blacks and whites were equally entitled to the natural rights of life, liberty, and property. Over the course of the 1850s Republicans became increasingly sympathetic to the idea that blacks and whites were equally entitled to the rights and privileges of citizenship. But before the Civil War there was little agreement among Republicans about the civil and political rights of African-Americans.[3] In this, as in so much else, Lincoln occupied the middle ground of the Republican Party. He was forceful and unambiguous in his insistence that blacks and whites were equally entitled to the natural rights to liberty and the pursuit of happiness, in particular the right to the fruits of labor. He was initially more equivocal about citizenship rights, but by the late 1850s was moving closer to the idea that the Constitution guaranteed the privileges and immunities of citizens without regard to race or color. But on issues that were traditionally the preserve of state majorities and legislatures, Lincoln openly deferred to prevailing racial prejudices. He made this clear in a few brief sentences he uttered at Charleston, Illinois, in September 1858. "I am not, nor ever have been, in favor of making voters or jurors of negroes," Lincoln said, "nor of qualifying them to hold office, nor to intermarry with white people." Until the last years of his life Lincoln was skeptical that whites and blacks could ever live together as equals in the United States and thought that the best solution was for African-Americans to voluntarily emigrate to a colony somewhere beyond the nation's borders.[4]

Lincoln's commitment to colonization was more a function of pessimism than of prejudice. Thomas Jefferson believed that blacks freed from slavery had to be colonized because their innate racial inferiority made them unfit to live as equals among whites. Lincoln never made such claims. Uninterested in the pseudoscience of race, he was far more disturbed by the seemingly intractable reality of white racial prejudice. Colonization was necessary, Lincoln seemed to believe, not because blacks were irredeemably inferior but because so many whites were irredeemably racist. Only by establishing a colony of their own could blacks enjoy the full measure of freedom and equality to which they were entitled—but which they could never expect in the United States. Yet for all his racial pessimism, Lincoln's commitment to colonization was less deeply seated than his hatred of slavery. His endorsements of colonization were erratic and often ambiguous, whereas his hatred of slavery was clear and at times uncharacteristically passionate. During the Civil War Lincoln's commitment to destroying slavery eclipsed and ultimately silenced his support for colonization.

In the middle of the nineteenth century, when the conflict over slavery was tearing the nation apart, Lincoln's views on race were controversial mostly because of how far he was willing to go in support of racial equality. His infamous remarks at Charleston don't help us understand this because they specify the limits rather than the extent of his commitment to equality for blacks and whites. What made the racial views of Lincoln and his fellow Republicans so controversial in their day—the reason they were so widely denounced as "Black Republicans"—has nothing to do with the forms of inequality they were willing to endorse and everything to do with how far they went in support of racial equality. Dip into any newspaper or pamphlet from the mid-nineteenth century, leaf through the record of congressional debates, and what screams out is not a racist consensus but a bitter conflict—ferocious, sustained, idealistic, and demagogic by turns—over whom Thomas Jefferson was talking about when he declared that "all men are created equal."

The debate over the reach of the Declaration of Independence was anything but abstract. Public officials who took one side in the debate endorsed one set of policies, and those who took the other side endorsed a radically different set of policies. The lives of millions of African-Americans could be radically transformed depending on which group of public officials acquired the power to implement its policies. Scratch beneath the surface of any debate about "race" in American history and sooner or later you're bound to discover a struggle for power—ultimately, political power.

Although the debate over racial equality was nationwide, it took place along two distinct registers. The first was the conflict pitting antislavery Northerners against proslavery Southerners. The second took place entirely within the North, ultimately pitting vehemently racist northern Democrats against moderately egalitarian northern Republicans. This was a recurring theme in the sectional crisis: on matters of race and slavery, the South united and the North divided. Southern leaders were virtually unanimous in defense of slavery and white supremacy, whereas northern leaders fought bitterly among themselves over both issues. The bitterness was conspicuous in Stephen A. Douglas's vulgar remarks about blacks and crocodiles, and Lincoln's heated attack upon them.

Actually, the dispute over racial equality between Lincoln and Douglas had begun years earlier, in 1854, when Lincoln came out of semiretirement and redefined himself as an antislavery politician. His first important antislavery speech, at Peoria, was the culmination of a series of speeches Lincoln had given as he followed Douglas around the state, attacking the senator for having sponsored the Nebraska bill that repealed the Missouri Compromise. Under Douglas's doctrine of popular sovereignty, territorial settlers would be free to legalize slavery if they wanted to. But that was a distorted version of popular sovereignty, Lincoln believed, because it gave whites the right to treat blacks as property, rather than as human beings. The issue was not the "doctrine of self-government"—we all agree with that, Lincoln said. The issue is "whether a negro is *not* or *is* a man. If he is *not* a man, why in that case, he who *is* a man may, as a matter of self-government, do just as he pleases with him. But if the negro *is* a man," Lincoln concluded, "why then my ancient faith teaches me that 'all men are created equal;' and there can be no moral right in connection with one man's making a slave of another." Lincoln then proceeded to quote at length from Jefferson's famed declaration that "all men are created equal," concluding that the "relation of masters and slaves is, PRO TANTO, a total violation of this principle." Lincoln was assuming that blacks and whites were equally human—that "the negro *is* a man"—and was therefore entitled to the fundamental rights promised to "all men" in the Declaration of Independence.[5] He even defied Stephen A. Douglas to recite the words of the Declaration of Independence with a racial qualification added. "I adhere to the Declaration of Independence," Lincoln said. "If Judge Douglas and his friends are not willing to stand by it, let them come up and amend it. Let them make it read that all men are created equal except negroes."[6]

Douglas did not shrink from the challenge. "Mr. Lincoln," he said, "reads from the Declaration of Independence that all men were created equal, and then asks how you can deprive a negro of that equality which God and the Declaration of Independence award to him. . . . But for my own part, I do not regard the negro as my equal. . . . I do not believe that the Almighty ever intended the negro to be the equal of the white man." The central question in the 1858 Illinois senate campaign, Douglas insisted, was "What is to be done with the free negro?" Lincoln dismissed this as a diversion—the real issue was slavery, and Douglas was avoiding the issue by attempting to shift the terms of debate from slavery to race.[7] Yet Lincoln invoked the same principle whether he was talking about slavery or racial equality. Denouncing slavery at Peoria in 1854, Lincoln insisted that "the *negro* is a man" and was therefore embraced by the principles of the Declaration.[8] Denouncing racism in New Haven in 1860, he insisted that "*slaves* are human beings; *men,* not property." Many of the things "stated about men in the Declaration of Independence apply to them as well as to us," Lincoln added. "I say, we think, most of us, that this Charter of Freedom applies to the slave as well as to ourselves."[9]

Whether he was attacking proslavery Southerners or racist Northerners, Lincoln tended to view his opponents in partisan terms as Democrats, though he clearly understood that by 1860 there were northern and southern "branches" of the Democratic Party. "Do you know of any Democrat," he asked, "of either branch of the party—do you know one who declares that he believes the Declaration of Independence has any application to the negro? Judge Taney declares that it has not, and Judge Douglas even vilifies me personally and scolds me roundly for saying that the Declaration applies to all men, and that negroes are men. [Cheers.] Is there a Democrat here who does not deny that the Declaration applies to a negro?" Yet Lincoln did not believe that Democrats said these things simply because they were racists. They were driven to the position, he argued, by the need to defend slavery. The "*whole Democratic party has deliberately taken negroes from the class of men and put them in the class of brutes*," he exclaimed. They have consciously set out to change public opinion "from where negroes are estimated as men to where they are estimated as mere brutes—as rightful property!" The Democracy was the party of racism, Lincoln believed, because it was the party of slavery.

By the 1850s the racial exception to the Declaration of Independence was a familiar theme in proslavery thought. As Alabama's J. L. M. Curry put it shortly after Lincoln was elected president, "The framers of the government engaged in no such sickly sentimentality or false philosophy as Lincoln and the Chicago platform avow. . . . They never dreamed that the Declaration of Independence included negroes, and that the negroes were entitled to freedom without reference to time and place."[10] Curry was not reviving the old, reactionary denunciation of Jefferson's ideal of human equality. There had always been such conservatives, north and south, men who despised egalitarianism in any form. But by the 1850s those types were hard to find, and most southern leaders who defended slavery accepted Jefferson's dictum in principle but made a crucial racial exception to it. That's what Chief Justice Roger Taney did in his 1857 Dred Scott decision. On Taney's reading, the Founders had never imagined that black people were included in the political nation they were creating. A bone-deep Jackson Democrat, Taney believed as firmly as anyone that "all men are created equal"; it's just that Thomas Jefferson meant the principle to apply only to whites. He meant all *white* men were created equal.

But Republicans insisted that Taney libeled the Founders when he claimed they had exempted blacks from their broad assertions of universal freedom. "Conceding the fact that the Declaration of Independence proclaimed a principle of Liberty," Charles Francis Adams argued in 1860, "the question has been made, to whom of God's creatures was it intended to apply. Was it all mankind, or only to a part? If to all mankind, of course it must have embraced those who were at the time in a state of slavery." But, Adams went on, Chief Justice Taney tells us that "when the fathers declared, in solemn tones, '*all* men to be created free and equal . . . ,' they intended to describe only the governing race,—that is, the white European race, of which they constituted a part." Taney had thereby reduced a great principle of general benefit to all mankind to "a mere domestic difference among the whites." This, Adams declared, was a "belittling" view of the Founders. "How mean they are made to appear in the boldness of their profession and the selfishness of their action."[11]

Republicans, in fact, commonly proclaimed their commitment to fundamental racial equality in their individual speeches as well as their official pronouncements. Article 2 of the 1860 Republican platform declared, for example, "[t]hat the maintenance of the principles promulgated in the Declaration of Independence and embodied in the Federal Constitution, 'That all men are created equal . . .' is essential to the preservation of our Republican institutions."[12] There was no racial exception in the platform. Unlike Democrats, when Republicans finished quoting the Declaration of Independence they added no devastating qualifier that limited the principle of universal freedom and the natural right to liberty to whites only. And it was obvious to everyone why this debate was so significant: the fate of millions of slaves rested on the outcome.

THE DEBATE OVER RACE had implications for the lives of hundreds of thousands of free blacks as well. The slavery controversy forced into public discussion a question about racial equality that, strictly speaking, had nothing to do with slaves: were free blacks citizens? Hardly anybody argued that slaves were citizens. A tradition stretching back through western history all the way to classical antiquity held that slaves were "noncitizens" by definition. And yet, from the Missouri crisis to the secession crisis, debates over slavery often raised the question of whether free blacks were citizens. Did the constitution submitted with Missouri's application for statehood, which excluded blacks from entering the state, violate the citizenship rights of free blacks? Did the South Carolina Seamen Act, and similar legislation in Louisiana—laws that provided that black sailors on ships from the North be held in jail until their ships departed from the state's ports— likewise deprive free blacks of the "privileges and immunities" guaranteed to all citizens? And most contentious of all, could the master's right to recapture fugitive slaves override northern state laws protecting the due process rights of their black citizens? Behind each of these specific questions lay a more general one about racial equality in the United States: were blacks entitled to the privileges and immunities the Constitution guaranteed to all citizens?

One of the first national debates over African-American citizenship erupted in Congress in the immediate aftermath of the Missouri Compromise. In late 1820, having been allowed to enter the Union as a slave state, Missouri submitted its new constitution to Congress for approval. Though the congressional debate over slavery in the previous session had been bitterly divisive, it was settled thanks to a compromise brokered by Henry Clay that allowed slavery into Missouri in return for a ban on slavery in the western territories north of Missouri's southern border and the simultaneous admission of Maine as a free state. A few months later Missourians drafted a new state constitution that generated another sharp division requiring yet another congressional compromise, brokered once again by Henry Clay. This second dispute, however, was provoked not by slavery but by a brief clause in Article III that would compel Missouri's legislature "to pass such laws as may be necessary . . . to prevent free negroes and mulattoes from coming to, and settling in this state, under any pretext whatsoever." Missouri's proposed constitution would thereby exclude all free blacks from entering the state.

Back in Congress a substantial number of senators and a majority in the House objected, citing the clause in the U.S. Constitution stating that "the citizens of one state shall be entitled to all the privileges and immunities of citizens of the several states." The Constitution nowhere specifies what those "privileges and immunities" were, but many Americans believed that they included the right to move freely from one state to another. Missouri's proposed constitution would thus deny one of the basic "privileges" to African-Americans migrating from a state in which they were recognized as citizens. What Missouri was proposing was "entirely repugnant to the Constitution," Senator James

Burrill of Rhode Island declared. Massachusetts recognizes "no distinction of color" among its citizens. "Can it be possible for Missouri," he asked, "consistently with the Constitution, to exclude any of those citizens of Massachusetts from the State?"[13]

South Carolina's Senator William Smith immediately disputed the premise that "free negroes and mulattoes are citizens." On the contrary, blacks were "never considered a part of the body politic," nor was the Declaration of Independence intended "for the blacks as well as the whites." It was hypocritical for northern senators to demand that blacks be recognized as citizens in Missouri, Smith argued, when their own states discriminated against blacks and often denied them the right to vote. Rhode Island should be especially ashamed to raise the issue of black citizenship, Smith added, given its own sordid history of involvement in the transatlantic slave trade. Maine's Senator John Holmes seconded Smith's point. Blacks were never intended to be citizens under the Constitution because, among other things, citizenship implied the right to vote and hold office—something northern states commonly denied to blacks.[14]

In response, the critics of Missouri's constitution argued that "sovereignty"—which included the right to vote and hold office—had never been one of the privileges and immunities of citizenship. Women and children were citizens, for example, though they could not vote or hold office. In his home state of Massachusetts, Senator Harrison Gray Otis explained, blacks were considered citizens and were therefore entitled to the rights and privileges of citizenship guaranteed by the Constitution, including "the right of protection in life, liberty, and property," the rights of due process, the right to own and inherit property, and the right to enter or leave the state freely. Missouri's constitution was unacceptable not because it deprived black citizens of the vote, but because it was "in palpable collision" with the Constitution's guarantee that privileges and immunities of citizens of one state were to be recognized by all states.[15]

The House debate over Missouri's constitution was, if anything, even more contentious than the Senate's. The committee report, introduced by Representative William Lowndes of South Carolina, acknowledged the dispute over black citizenship, but argued that there was no agreement among states about what things counted as "privileges and immunities" under the Constitution. Traditionally, each state was free to make that determination for itself, Lowndes noted, and Congress had never before required a state applying for admission to recognize the citizenship of blacks. It would be best, he argued, for Congress to uphold that precedent now. Lowndes even suggested that it was none of Congress's business to be evaluating the constitutional validity of this or that clause of a proposed state charter; those were matters for the courts to decide.[16]

In a lengthy reply, Congressman John Sergeant of Pennsylvania insisted that the power to review a proposed state constitution was "emphatically ours"—that is, Congress's. "Suppose," he wondered, Missouri's constitution "had said that no free *white* citizen of the United States should come and reside in Missouri—was there any gentleman who would say that, with such a provision, Missouri ought to be admitted to the Union?" He disputed Lowndes's claim that the privileges and immunities clause of the Constitution was "so difficult of construction that this House could not decide whether or not it had been violated in a given case." Surely there could be no disagreement that the Constitution protected "the humblest and lowest right enjoyed by a free man . . . to go into any other State, to return, or to remain there." If Missouri's constitution "excluded altogether" any free man "who is a citizen of another State of this Union," Sergeant declared, "then it is impossible to reconcile that constitution with the Constitution of the United States."[17] Massachusetts, New York, and even North Carolina all recognized free blacks as citizens, he noted, and it was "not necessary they should have a right to vote" to be citizens. Half the white men in America were excluded from the vote by various property qualifications, "yet no one would deny them to be citizens of those States." All that was being asked for in this case, Sergeant pleaded, was that free African-Americans be allowed to enjoy "the humble simple privilege of locomotion . . . a right indispensable to citizenship."

On two separate occasions the House of Representatives rejected Missouri's constitution on the grounds that it deprived black citizens of the privileges and immunities guaranteed to all citizens by the Constitution. The pattern of voting was sharply sectional. The overwhelming majority of northern congressmen, from states that recognized free blacks as citizens, refused to accept the Missouri restriction. Once again Henry Clay had to step in to broker another compromise. Missouri promised not to deprive any citizens of their rights, but the ban on black emigration remained in place because Missouri did not recognize blacks as citizens.

As with so many such compromises, Clay had cobbled together the votes of a nearly unanimous South and a northern minority, to defeat the majority of northern congressmen who held out for the privileges and immunities of free black citizens.

Black citizenship was once again the issue in the dispute between northern and southern states over the legitimacy of the Negro-Seamen Act adopted by South Carolina in 1822. The law required the automatic imprisonment of all free black sailors working on vessels arriving in Charleston harbor, until such time as the vessels left port. A few years later Louisiana passed a similar law. Though designed to protect slavery from the subversive presence of free blacks, these laws were a form of racial discrimination against free black sailors. Merchants from England and the northern states protested the imprisonment of their employees, but southern courts routinely upheld the legality of the seamen's statutes. In 1824 the U.S. attorney general, William Wirt, ruled that the South Carolina law was incompatible with the treaties governing trade relations under the law of nations. This meant that black sailors on foreign ships could no longer be imprisoned. But African-American sailors working on American ships could be. Because Congress washed its hands of the business, the debate over the citizenship rights of black sailors took place between the contending states.

In the 1830s the Massachusetts legislature took up the cause, defending black sailors who, though "citizens of this Commonwealth," were nevertheless subjected to fines, imprisonment, and enslavement in southern ports. Massachusetts merchants protested as well, for their vessels were repeatedly stripped of black workers upon entering the ports of Savannah, Mobile, Charleston, and New Orleans. In 1842 they signed a memorial asking Congress to "render effectual the privileges of citizenship secured by the Constitution." After years of fruitless protests Massachusetts sent an emissary to South Carolina hoping to negotiate a settlement, but instead the Carolina legislature passed a series of resolutions denying that blacks were "citizens of the United States" under the Constitution and urging the governor to "expel the emissary sent by Massachusetts."[18]

The dispute over the Seamen Act stretched from the late 1820s into the 1840s, a period when party leaders made concerted efforts to keep slavery out of national politics. Rightly fearful of the disruptive potential of the slavery issue, Whigs and Democrats—who were vying for votes in the North as well as the South—struggled to suppress all talk of slavery, and with it all talk of free black citizenship, at the national level.[19]

IT WAS DURING those same decades, however, that northern legislatures passed a series of laws designed to protect their black citizens against the threat of kidnapping posed by slave catchers attempting to recapture fugitive slaves. A rapidly emerging majority of northern voters accepted the abolitionist argument that because slavery was strictly a state institution, the fugitive-slave clause of the Constitution should be enforced by states, not the federal government. If northern states chose to enforce the clause by guaranteeing all accused fugitives their day in court, those states should be free to do so. If northern courts operated from the presumption that all men were free, putting the burden of proof on slave catchers to demonstrate otherwise, again those courts should be free to do so. For most northern opponents of slavery, the best way to thwart the fugitive-slave clause was by defending the privileges and immunities of free black citizens in a series of statutes known collectively as the personal liberty laws.

In 1850, in an attempt to thwart the northern personal liberty laws, Congress passed a new Fugitive Slave Act giving federal commissioners the power to adjudicate fugitive-slave cases within the northern states. A majority of northern congressmen and senators opposed the 1850 law but they were defeated by a familiar alliance between a united South and a northern minority. The Fugitive Slave Act overruled the presumption of citizenship for free blacks in the northern states by preventing those states from recognizing the due process rights of accused fugitives.

Despite the increasing popularity of the abolitionist argument that the fugitive-slave clause should be enforced by the states, not all antislavery politicians agreed. Some, including radicals like Oliver P. Morton and moderates like Abraham Lincoln, believed that the fugitive-slave clause did create a *federal* enforcement obligation. But in so doing, it also gave the federal government the right to establish the legal procedures by which that obligation was met. For men like Morton and Lincoln, this meant that the federal government should recognize the same due process rights that northern states required for the rendition of fugitive slaves. As Lincoln put it in Peoria in 1854, a proper fugitive-slave law "should not, in its stringency, be more likely to carry a free man into slavery, than our ordinary criminal laws are to hang an innocent one."[20] Even with federal enforcement of the fugitive-slave clause, then, the due process rights to which all citizens were entitled should be automatically extended to all blacks accused of being fugitive slaves.

Such reasoning found no place in most southern courts, where the protection of racial slavery largely determined the legal standing of free blacks. As a judge in Georgia put it in 1853, "the act of manumission confers no other right but that of freedom from the domination of the master, and the limited liberty of locomotion—it does not and cannot confer citizenship, nor any of the powers, civil or political, incident to citizenship." The reason for this, the judge explained, was that "the social and civil degradation, resulting from the taint of blood, adheres to the descendants of Ham in this country, like the poisoned tunic of Nessus."[21] Blacks were enslaved because they were racially inferior to whites and the fact of their inferiority could not be altered by their emancipation.

These two conflicting presumptions about black citizenship, simmering for decades, boiled over into a full-scale national debate in 1857, thanks to Chief Justice Roger Taney's decision in the Dred Scott case. Whatever privileges individual states might choose to grant as a courtesy to their black residents, Taney argued, they bore no relevance to the status of blacks under the U.S. Constitution. Taney went on to define national citizenship in terms so restrictive that no black person would qualify. Rehearsing arguments voiced decades earlier during the Missouri controversy, Taney declared that blacks had not been part of the "political nation" at the time of its founding and could therefore never be citizens of the United States. Hence the privileges and immunities clause of the Constitution had no bearing on African-Americans.[22]

Two weeks after Taney published his decision, Lincoln criticized the chief justice for insisting "at great length that negroes were no part of the people who made, or for whom was made, the Declaration of Independence, or the Constitution."[23] Indeed, the basic thrust of Taney's ruling, Lincoln said, "is that a negro cannot be a citizen."[24] The Court's purpose was "to deprive the negro, in every possible event, of the benefit of that provision of the United States Constitution which declares that 'the citizens of each State shall be entitled to all privileges and immunities of citizens in the several States.'"[25] In his 1858 "House Divided" speech Lincoln again denounced Taney's claim "that no negro slave, imported as such from Africa, and no descendant of such slave can ever be a citizen of any State, in the sense of that term as used in the Constitution of the United States."[26] Lincoln anticipated, correctly as it turned out, that his speech would set the terms for his upcoming series of debates with Stephen Douglas.

Lincoln says he is opposed to the Dred Scott decision because it "deprives the negro of the rights and privileges of citizenship," Douglas declared in their very first debate. "I ask you," Douglas went on, "are you in favor of conferring upon the negro the rights and privileges of citizenship?" If you "desire negro citizenship, if you desire to allow them to come into the State and settle with the white man, if you desire them to vote on an equality with yourselves, and to make them eligible to office, to serve on juries, and to adjudge your rights, then support Mr. Lincoln and the Black Republican party, who are in favor of the citizenship of the negro."[27] There was no stopping him. "I hold that a negro is not and never ought to be a citizen of the United States," Douglas declared at Jonesboro. "I do not believe that the Almighty made the negro capable of self-government."[28]

Lincoln wavered in the face of Douglas's prodigious assault but he never retracted his original claim, and by 1860 Lincoln was openly denouncing his victorious rival for "brutalizing" African-Americans in ways that helped legitimate the idea that black people could be treated as property. In his first inaugural address, in March 1861, Lincoln openly repudiated the Dred Scott decision. He would revise the Fugitive Slave Act of 1850, Lincoln said, so as to ensure that no accused runaways would be deprived of "the privileges and immunities" that the Constitution promised to every citizen.[29]

By then seven southern states had already seceded from the Union citing, among other reasons, the Republican Party's commitment to racial equality. Secessionists roundly denounced Lincoln for advocating "the dangerous dogma" that "the negro is the equal of the white man."[30] The state of Georgia justified secession on the ground that Republicans advocated the "prohibition of slavery in the Territories, hostility to it everywhere, [and] the equality of the black and white races."[31] Mississippi's declaration of secession explained that the Republican Party seeks to "extinguish" slavery everywhere and "advocates negro equality, socially and politically."[32]

But in saying these things secessionists did not repudiate the Declaration of Independence as they had long understood it. They saw no contradiction between Thomas Jefferson's promise of fundamental human equality and Jefferson Davis's commitment to white supremacy. Even South Carolina, in its declaration of the causes justifying secession, repeatedly invoked the Declaration of Independence and at the same time denounced the northern states for "elevating to citizenship, persons who, by the supreme law of the land, are incapable of becoming citizens."[33] Texas secessionists went even further, actually paraphrasing Jefferson's words, but adding the all-important racial exception. They assailed the northern states for "proclaiming the debasing doctrine of equality of all men, irrespective of race or color." By contrast, the Texans explained: "We hold as undeniable truths that the governments of the various States, and of the confederacy itself, were established exclusively by the white race, for themselves and their posterity . . . [t]hat in this free government all white men are and of right ought to be entitled to equal civil and political rights."[34]

THE REPUBLICAN PARTY was not a treasury of virtue. It did not advocate the kind of social and political equality that many radical abolitionists courageously endorsed. In fact, Republicans didn't much like talking about race. But they couldn't avoid the questions raised by their own commitment to slavery's ultimate extinction. How could slavery be right if "all men" were created equal and blacks were "men"? Where in the Constitution does it say that the privileges and immunities of citizenship are restricted by race or color?

Why is a black woman any less entitled to the fruits of her labor than a white man? It was impossible to question slavery without raising questions about racial inequality. Running through the debate over slavery was a corresponding debate over the place of African-Americans in the United States—a debate in which Democrats denied that blacks had any natural right to freedom or any claim to the privileges and immunities of citizenship, and in which Republicans insisted that freedom was a universal right and that African-Americans were citizens of their states and therefore of their nation. The irreconcilable conflict over slavery was, inescapably, an irreconcilable conflict over racial equality.

BY THE LATE 1850s a new Republican Party committed to slavery's ultimate extinction had sprung up in the northern states. Republicans adopted many of the principles and policies of the more radical antislavery movement. Freedom was the "natural" condition of every human being, and of everyone living under the direct authority of the Constitution. Free labor was superior to enslaved labor, both ethically as well as materially. It was "unnatural" for one human being to hold another as property. Only positive state and local laws could override the presumption of freedom. The federal government had no power to interfere with those state policies, but it was free to adopt policies designed to surround the South with a cordon of freedom until, like a scorpion surrounded by fire, slavery would put itself to death—gradually, and without war.

As the threat of secession and war loomed ever more ominously, however, Republicans began to talk of an entirely different means of attacking slavery—military emancipation. Freeing slaves in wartime was an ancient practice, recognized by nearly all American statesmen as legitimate under the laws of war. Although widely accepted, military emancipation had never been central to the abolitionist agenda, much less to the Republican Party platform. And yet, by 1863 it was the most conspicuous feature of the Union's broad antislavery effort. As the Confederacy recoiled in horror, the irreconcilable conflict over slavery became an irreconcilable conflict over the laws of war.

4

The Wars over Wartime Emancipation

On November 26, 1862, Jefferson Davis unleashed the first of many scathing attacks on the Emancipation Proclamation, which was scheduled for release the following New Year's Day. Military emancipation of the sort adopted by federal policy makers, Davis declared, demonstrated the Union's "manifest distrust of success in warfare conducted according to the usages of civilized nations." Beginning in the earliest months of the war, Union policy makers argued that military emancipation was a familiar exercise of the federal government's constitutional war powers—grounded in historical precedent and sanctioned by the law of nations.[1] Davis denied this. By invading the southern states and emancipating their slaves, he insisted, the Union was violating the very laws of war Lincoln invoked in his defense. Military emancipation would "inflict on the non-combatant population of the Confederate States all the horrors of a servile war."[2] Northerners thought freeing slaves was a legitimate, effective, and morally justified weapon in their effort to suppress the southern rebellion, but to Confederates military emancipation was a repudiation of the rules of civilized warfare, a descent into the "barbarism" of past ages. Because they tended to see slavery as the theft of the property all humans had in themselves, Union policy makers often saw emancipation as the restoration of the slave's long-denied property rights. But southern leaders argued that slaves were private property, no different from tables and chairs; to them emancipation was a monstrous violation of the principle that civilian property was immune to depredation by invading armies. The irreconcilable conflict over slavery was also an irreconcilable conflict over military emancipation.

It was not the first such conflict in American history.

ON NOVEMBER 7, 1775, the royal governor of Virginia, John Murray, the Earl of Dunmore, issued his own emancipation proclamation inviting rebel-owned slaves to claim their freedom by escaping to his lines and joining the British in their effort to suppress the quickening American rebellion. Dunmore declared "free" all indentured servants and blacks "appertaining to Rebels" who were "willing to bear arms, they joining His Majesty's Troops." Dunmore's proclamation was only the beginning. As the War of Independence shifted into the southern states, large numbers of slaves ran to the British claiming their freedom. On June 3, 1780, the British commander, Henry Clinton, issued a proclamation that was more expansive than Dunmore's, promising freedom to all rebel-owned slaves who came within his lines, whether or not they offered their military service to His Majesty's forces. By the time the War of Independence ended with Lord Cornwallis's surrender at Yorktown, perhaps 5 percent of the blacks enslaved in the southern colonies had escaped to the English—five thousand from Virginia and Maryland and another thirteen thousand from Georgia and the Carolinas. In all perhaps twenty thousand blacks sided with the British during the American Revolution.[3]

But they were not the only slaves freed by the war. The Americans had responded to the British in kind. In February 1778, Rhode Island offered freedom to "such slaves as should be willing to enter into the service" of the Continental army. The legislators cited the "frequent precedents of the wisest, the freest, and bravest nations having liberated their slaves, and enlisted them as soldiers in defense of their country." Other states followed suit. Eventually New Hampshire, Massachusetts, New York, and even Maryland offered freedom to slaves who served in the Continental army "for the duration" of the war. Virginia freed five hundred slaves in return for military service. Even Congress endorsed the practice. In March 1779, the representatives in Philadelphia passed a resolution urging South Carolina and Georgia to offer emancipation to as many as three thousand slaves who enlisted in the Continental army and fought for the duration of the war. Their masters would be compensated, and when the war was over each of the former slaves would be given fifty dollars.[4] Freeing your own slaves raised no special issues involving the laws of war, but it had two important implications for the way Americans talked about the practice. First, compensation removed the stigma of theft from military emancipation, and, second, it silenced those who equated offers of freedom with incitement to servile insurrection.

In 1776, only months after Lord Dunmore issued his proclamation, patriot leaders skewered King George for having—as Thomas Jefferson put it in the Declaration of Independence—"excited domestic insurrections amongst us." But that charge quickly disappeared from the colonists' litany of complaints once the Americans themselves began offering slaves freedom in return for military service. By the 1790s there was a broad consensus among Americans about the status of slavery in war and peace: it was perfectly legitimate under the laws of war to free enemy slaves, especially in return for military service and, once freed, they could never be reenslaved—unless reenslavement of a specific group of people was clearly required by the terms of the treaty ending the war.[5]

This was a diplomatic variant of the *Somerset* principle, enunciated by Lord Mansfield from the Court of King's Bench in 1772—at least as Americans came to understand that principle. Somerset was a Virginia slave who had been taken to England by his master and, once there, sued for his freedom. Mansfield ruled that only "positive" laws creating slavery could override the "natural" condition of freedom. Such laws existed in the colonies but not in England, hence the slave Somerset was freed once he set foot on British soil. A similar principle applied in cases of war and peace. Under the laws of war emancipated slaves were said to have been restored to their "natural" condition of freedom and could not be reenslaved unless a treaty unambiguously obliged the emancipators to withdraw the freedom granted to slaves during the war.[6]

Because virtually all American statesmen subscribed to these precepts by the late eighteenth century, disputes over wartime emancipation nearly always came down to questions about the language of the treaty itself rather than abstract claims about the laws of war: Did the treaty protect emancipated people from reenslavement, or did it require the "restitution" of slaves to their former owners? Which slaves were to be restored and which were beyond restitution? Did the treaty prescribe compensation when slaves were not returned to their rightful owners? Could these questions be answered by the "plain sense" of the treaty, or was the language ambiguous and therefore open to conflicting interpretations? If the language was unclear, should disputes be resolved by arbitration, or by resort to the general principles of the law of nations? These were the terms of the debate over the fate of the thousands of slaves who had escaped to the British during the War of Independence but who were still in the United States when the war ended. Nobody doubted that the law of nations—from which the laws of war were derived—entitled belligerents to free slaves in wartime. The question was always: what was required by the treaty that ended the war?[7]

THE FIRST OF MANY such questions arose in 1783, only months after England and America agreed to the Treaty of Paris that formally ended the War of Independence. In November 1782, at the very end of the peace process, one of the American negotiators, Henry Laurens of South Carolina, suggested the addition of the single crucial reference to slaves in the "Definitive Treaty of Peace" that both sides were about to sign. Laurens was a wealthy planter and slave trader who had recently been released from prison in the Tower of London and arrived in France to join the American delegation only after the bulk of the treaty had been drafted. His additional wording, incorporated into Article VII, required British forces in the United States to begin their evacuation "with all convenient speed, and without causing any destruction, or carrying away any negroes or other property of the American inhabitants."[8]

What did that mean? "Negroes or other property" clearly referred to slaves; nobody doubted that. But what, if anything, did the clause require the departing British to do? The record of the peace negotiations is of no help because Laurens played almost no role in them, and the draft of the treaty he read upon arriving in Paris contained no reference to slavery. In the preceding months of negotiations Congress at one point threatened to demand compensation for emancipated slaves if the British did not drop their own demand that American loyalists be compensated for the property they had lost during the war. When the British backed down, the congressional threat was withdrawn. As a result, the Americans never demanded that the British either return slaves carried away *during* the war or compensate their owners for those losses. The clause Laurens inserted into Article VII did not change this. In preventing the British from carrying away slaves *during the evacuation,* it left free and unmolested the thousands of slaves already carried away to England, Canada, or the Caribbean. That much everyone understood. Article VII referred only to "negroes and other property" still in the United States at the time the war ended, but there was sharp disagreement about what the treaty said about them.

The British claimed that they had already emancipated the slaves who had come within their lines during the war and that Article VII could not possibly oblige them to reenslave people to whom they had promised freedom. Thus in the British reading, the treaty applied only to slaves who continued to come within British lines after the treaty was signed, for the power to emancipate ended when the war itself ended. By contrast, Americans claimed that the thousands of blacks under the protection of the British were still slaves because they had not yet been carried away beyond the borders of the United States. Those people remained the "property" of "American inhabitants" and in signing the treaty the British forfeited their right to carry such property away. Nothing in the wording of Article VII could resolve this dispute, nor could the record of negotiations in Paris settle the issue because there was no record. As a result, the disagreement over the meaning of Article VII dragged on for more than a decade.

During the summer of 1782, while the peace negotiations were underway in France, British General Alexander Leslie, who oversaw the evacuation of Charleston, repeatedly expressed his reluctance to leave behind the thousands of slaves who had come within his lines during the war. "There are many negroes who have been very useful, both at the Siege of Savannah and here," Leslie wrote. "Some of them have been guides and for their loyalty have been promised freedom." Leslie understood that he was obliged to turn away slaves who escaped to his lines *after* Cornwallis's surrender at Yorktown. But those who had come during the war, especially those who had assisted the British military effort, could not "in justice be abandoned to the merciless resentment of their former masters." Leslie established a commission to distinguish between slaves who had been legally emancipated during wartime and those who would have to be returned. But mutual mistrust and recrimination between the British and the Americans undermined the commission's work. When the British evacuated Charleston in December 1782, they "carried away" thousands of emancipated blacks, along with thousands of slaves owned by loyalists escaping retribution at the hands of the victorious patriots.[9]

Perhaps in response to the evacuation of thousands of blacks from South Carolina and Georgia, Congress passed a resolution urging General George Washington to secure the return of any slaves still under the purview of the British troops awaiting evacuation from New York. The resolution "instructed" Washington "to make proper arrangement with the commander in chief of the British forces," Sir Guy Carleton, "for obtaining delivery of all negroes and other property of the inhabitants of the United States in possession of the British forces."[10] It was Carleton who had advised Leslie to distinguish between slaves who had been promised freedom during the war and those who came within British lines after the war ended. Carleton may well have been influenced by Maurice Morgann, an avid supporter of emancipation within Carleton's entourage, but whatever his reasons, they led to a famous exchange with Washington at Orangeburg, New York, on May 6, 1782.[11]

Washington pointed out that slaves were still being carried away on British ships as they evacuated and he demanded the return of all slaves still within the boundaries of the United States at the moment the war ended. He accused the British of bad faith, of violating the supposedly plain language of Article VII of the treaty that had been ratified only months before. (He also asked Carleton to "look out" for some of his own slaves who had escaped to the British.) But Carleton was adamant. He noted that most of the blacks within British lines had already been freed by the time he arrived in New York. Carleton had neither the authority nor the inclination to reenslave them and insisted that the British signatories to the treaty could not possibly have intended him to perpetrate such a "dishonorable Violation of the public faith." He was willing to keep a register of the blacks who were evacuated from New York with the British in case future negotiations led to an agreement to compensate the former masters, but the slaves to whom the British had promised freedom would remain free, whether or not the masters were compensated. As Leslie had done in Charleston, Carleton set up a commission to record the hundreds of names of the freed people who left with the British during the evacuation. Many hundreds more departed on private ships and could never be accounted for. Excluded from the roster—beyond either restitution or compensation—were the thousands who had already left the country before the war ended.

Carleton's position quickly became the official British response to repeated American demands for restitution or compensation. All slaves who had been promised freedom prior to November 30, 1782, the day the peace treaty was signed in Paris, would remain free. Article VII, the British insisted, applied only to slaves who came within their lines after that date. But the Americans considered the date irrelevant; to them what mattered was the fact that "negroes or other property" were still being carried away by the British after the war ended, during the evacuation. This, slaveholders claimed, was a clear violation of Article VII.

The dispute dragged on into the postwar years. When the British complained of American violations of the treaty, Congress authorized the secretary of foreign affairs, John Jay, to prepare a detailed response. His report, submitted in October 1786, distinguished between "*three* Classes" of slaves. The first comprised those who "in the course of the War were captured and disposed of as booty by the Enemy." The restriction in Article VII "cannot," Jay concluded, "be construed to extend to, and comprehend the *first* Class." Slaves carried away by the British before the war ended had been legitimately emancipated and the Americans were not asking for either restitution or compensation. The "*Second* Class" of slaves included those who, at the war's end, remained with their owners but within British lines. Those slaves did not qualify as "booty" under the laws of war and could not therefore be "carried away" by the British once the war was over. Nor could the third class of slaves cited by Jay—those who had escaped from their owners and were inside British lines, though still on American soil, at the time the war ended. The dispute between England and the United States concerned this last group. Jay concluded that the British had, in fact, violated Article VII by carrying away "negroes or other property" still on American soil when the war ended.[12] If he had stopped there, his report would have been nothing more than a familiar reiteration of what was, in 1786, the standard American position.

But Jay did not stop there. Having provided Congress with his view of the proper legal construction of the treaty, he went on to argue that the treaty itself was immoral because Article VII called for the reenslavement of people who had already been freed. Imagine if France and Algiers went to war, Jay said, and thousands of American slaves escaped to French lines anticipating their freedom. "[W]hat would Congress, and indeed the world, think and say of France, if, on making peace with Algiers, [they] would give up those American Slaves to their former Algerine Masters? Is there any other difference between these two cases," Jay asked, beyond the fact "that the American Slaves at Algiers are *white* people, whereas the African Slaves at New York were *Black* people?" No doubt the British had violated the letter of the treaty when they evacuated slaves from New York after the war ended, but did the Americans really want to press the point? It was wrong for the Americans to have demanded the return of those slaves, and the British should never have agreed to the demand. Faced with the consequences of their agreement and forced to choose between obeying the law and abiding by the dictates of morality, the British chose "to keep faith with the slaves by carrying them away." The simplest way to resolve the conflict, Jay concluded, was for the Americans to drop their demand that the slaves be returned, and instead accept monetary compensation from the British.[13]

Southerners were scandalized by Jay's report and persisted in their claim that England had violated the Treaty of Paris by carrying away slaves during the evacuation. But they were also forced to acknowledge that, at that point, there was no hope that their slaves would ever be returned. However reluctantly, they followed Jay's lead and demanded compensation instead.

NOT SURPRISINGLY, southern leaders were still skeptical when, ten years later, President Washington appointed Jay—by then the chief justice of the Supreme Court—to oversee a new round of treaty negotiations with Great Britain. Among the issues Jay was sent to London to discuss was England's continued refusal to compensate American masters for the slaves "carried away" during the evacuation, allegedly in violation of Article VII of the Treaty of Paris.

In London Jay quickly discovered that the British were immovable on the subject. As Lord Grenville explained, Article VII merely required that the British evacuation "be made without depredation." This meant that "no alteration" in the status of either British or American property could take place once the treaty had been signed. But the slaves who had already escaped from the Americans had become *"British* property," Grenville insisted, "and, therefore, ceasing to be *American* property, the exportation thereof was not inhibited" by the 1783 treaty. Those slaves came into British lines having been promised their freedom. To demand that the promise of liberty be broken and that the freed people be returned to slavery, Grenville said, was to give Article VII "a construction which, being *odius,* could not be supported by the known and established rules for construing treaties." On this point, Jay declared, "we could not agree."[14]

But it was also clear to both Jay and Grenville that their negotiations could easily bog down in claims and counterclaims about the other side's putative violations of the 1783 treaty. "It then became advisable to quit those topics," Jay reported. Both parties had pressing issues to discuss regarding the carrying trade with the West Indies, unpaid debts, the status of British troops in the western territories, and especially the navigation of the Mississippi. Rather than allow the negotiations to collapse, both Jay and Grenville abandoned any further discussion of compensation for slaves carried away during the British evacuation of America a decade earlier.

Secretary of State Edmund Randolph was dismayed by the report of British intransigence, and in a long letter to Jay he spelled out what quickly became the prevailing view among those demanding compensation for slaves. Randolph did not dispute the right of the British to confiscate "moveable" property under the laws of war, nor did he even hint that in offering slaves freedom the British had "excited domestic insurrections." Instead, Randolph claimed that abstract principles of the laws of war were rendered irrelevant once the British agreed to the treaty of 1783. "That a property is acquired in moveables as soon as they come within the power of the enemy, is acknowledged," Randolph explained. "But it will not be denied that rights, even in moveables acquired by war, may, by the treaty of peace, be renounced." Contrary to Grenville's claim, there was nothing odious in a treaty that required the British to return the property they had acquired during the war. "What is more customary than for nations to surrender rights?" Randolph asked. "What more common than for them to surrender, on a peace, rights acquired purely and solely through a war?"[15]

Without the treaty, then, the British position had merit under the laws of war. But by agreeing to Article VII, Randolph claimed, the British formally surrendered their claim to slave "property" still within U.S. borders at the end of the war. As for the slaves themselves, Randolph acknowledged that the war had given them "the chance of liberation. They were covered in their flight from their masters by the operation of war." But the slaves "must have been conscious" that "what the war gave, might, by a peace, be taken away." According to Randolph, Article VII called for reenslaving some of those he conceded had been legitimately freed by the war. Grenville's claim that the Treaty of Paris merely prohibited any further emancipation was spurious because, as Randolph read it, Article VII plainly and unambiguously called for the return of "negroes or other property" still on American soil when the war ended.[16]

Jay wouldn't budge. "We could not agree about the negroes," he repeated to Randolph. "Was that a good reason for breaking up the negotiations?"[17] He returned from London to New York in late May 1795, bearing a treaty that made no mention of slavery, effectively conceding that the British would not compensate American masters for slaves carried away during their evacuation more than a decade earlier. President Washington submitted the treaty to the Senate where it was approved by a vote of 20 to 10—just reaching the two-thirds majority required—and returned to

Washington for ratification. By then, Randolph, the stron-
gest opponent of the treaty in the cabinet, had resigned.
Alexander Hamilton, the secretary of the treasury and an
enthusiastic supporter of the treaty, leaped into the void
created by Randolph's departure and prepared a lengthy
memo that, among other things, defended the British interpretation of Article VII of the Treaty of Paris.

Hamilton's memo amounted to the first major American
defense of military emancipation under the laws of war. He
conceded that in "seducing away our negroes during the
War" the British had behaved in an "infamous" manner, but
this was little more than a conciliatory fig leaf, for Hamilton
went on to argue that Britain's behavior was entirely consistent with enlightened rules of war. Moreover, if it was "infamous" to emancipate slaves in wartime, to reenslave those
who had already been emancipated "would have been still
more infamous." The British had a point when they described
American demands for the return of slaves as odious. "Odious things are not favored in the interpretation of Treaties,"
Hamilton argued "and though the restoration of *property* is a
favored thing yet the surrender of persons to *slavery* is an odious thing." In all of this Hamilton claimed to be "speaking in
the language of the law of nations." He cited Emmerich de
Vattel's argument that because the execution of prisoners of
war was no longer legitimate, enslavement as an alternative
to execution had also become illegitimate. He quoted Hugo
Grotius to the effect that masters could only recover slaves
they "actually held" or who were "easily obtainable."[18]

Hamilton then examined the validity of the British claim
that the treaty itself did not require them to return slaves to

their masters. By referring to "negroes or other property," Article VII "puts negroes cows horses & all other articles of *property* on the same footing." Echoing John Jay's 1786 report to Congress, and even Randolph's letter to Jay, Hamilton concluded that slave "property" was legitimate "booty" of war. Thus, the slaves had become "the absolute *property of the Captors.*" But the "Captor" was thereafter within his rights to emancipate the slaves "in his possession." Once the slaves had been granted their freedom, Hamilton asked, "could the grant be recalled? Could the British government stipulate the surrender of men made free to slavery?" Could the ambiguous words of Article VII be made to bear such an "odious" construction when a different construction, one more attuned to "the rights of humanity," was readily available? After all, the treaty could reasonably be read as merely prohibiting the "carrying away" of property "not changed by the laws of war." There was no escaping the implication of Hamilton's argument. The slaves within British lines had already been emancipated, their status as property had been "changed by the laws of war." They were no longer "property" as contemplated by the treaty. This was how the British interpreted Article VII. We may not agree with them, Hamilton concluded, but they had raised "a well founded doubt as to the true legal construction."[19] This was a crucial point for Hamilton: Article VII was anything but unambiguous. It did not clearly require the British to compensate American masters for the slaves they had legally emancipated during the war.

On August 14, 1795, a few weeks after Hamilton submitted his memo to the president, Washington ratified

the treaty. When the text of the document was leaked to
the press shortly before the ratification, it immediately
provoked a raging debate. Once again Hamilton jumped
into the fray, abandoning the posture of evenhandedness
he had affected in his memo to the president. In a series
of essays in Jay's defense, published under the pseudonym
"Camilus," Hamilton relentlessly assailed Randolph's claim
that the British had breached the supposedly unambiguous requirements of Article VII of the Paris treaty.

Hamilton began by rehearsing familiar Enlightenment
arguments tending to favor emancipation under the laws
of war. Slaves were not like property "in land," which must
always be returned to its owners when the enemy evacuates.
If the slave states chose to define slaves as "personal property"
indistinguishable from "horses, cattle, and other moveables,"
Hamilton wrote, they must therefore accept that under the
laws of war slaves are "liable to become booty—and belong
to the enemy as soon as they came into his hands." The new
owners were then free "to set them at liberty." Even Randolph had conceded this point, claiming instead that the
treaty later superseded the laws of war. But Hamilton went in
another direction. In his memo to the president Hamilton
had wondered whether it was reasonable to demand that the
British return free men to slavery. Now, in print, he declared
flatly that the British had no power to reenslave anyone. The
grant of freedom "was irrevocable—restitution was impossible," Hamilton said, for there was "[n]othing in the laws
of Nations or in those of Great Britain" that could authorize
taking away "liberty once granted to a human being."[20] This
is where Vattel's point implicitly sustained Hamilton's: once

civilized nations banned the execution of prisoners of war, there was no longer any justification for enslavement as an alternative to execution, which effectively meant there was no justification left for any form of enslavement. It followed that the British could not legally enslave people they had already emancipated under the laws of war.

Hamilton softened his earlier suggestion that British wartime emancipation was "infamous" and instead asserted more forcefully that freeing slaves was accepted practice under the widely understood laws of war. However "dishonorable" Britain's "illiberal species of warfare" might have been, he wrote, "there is no ground to say that the strict rules of war did not warrant it." Hamilton now stated clearly what he had previously implied: the "stipulation" in the Treaty of Paris refers to the *property* of *American* inhabitants, but "the negroes in question by the laws of war had lost that character"—they were no longer property and no longer owned by Americans. "They were therefore not within the stipulation." Moreover, those now demanding compensation were violating the standard rules governing international agreements. "In the interpretation of Treaties," Hamilton explained, "things *odious* or *immoral* are not to be presumed." To reenslave a person who had been freed by the legitimate rules of war "is as *odious* and *immoral* a thing as can be conceived." If there was any ambiguity in the wording of a treaty, the "odiousness" of reenslavement must "incline" against that "effect." The more reasonable interpretation of the treaty was that, far from requiring the reenslavement of those who had already been freed, it merely prohibited any further emancipation once the war was over. On one issue the treaty was unambiguous, Hamilton argued: it said nothing at all about "compensation for the negroes" carried away.[21]

Hamilton made no claims to originality. Some of the leading lawyers in America, he said, had always subscribed to his interpretation of the Treaty of Paris. Nevertheless, his defense of military emancipation lived on to become, arguably, the single most influential summation of the antislavery interpretation of the laws of war published in the United States before the Civil War. Within months of its appearance Hamilton's essay became a flashpoint in the debate over the Jay treaty that consumed the House of Representatives for nearly two months in the spring of 1796. Critics of the treaty denounced the essay's not-so-anonymous author, Camilus. Jay's defenders repeated Hamilton's arguments, paraphrased his sentences, and cited the same sources Hamilton cited.

Given the sweeping scope of Hamilton's essay and the intensity of the controversy it aroused, it is remarkable how narrowly his opponents framed their replies. The extended House debate gave the critics of the Jay treaty ample opportunity to say their piece.[22] Yet rather than launch a broad argument in defense of compensation, critics of the treaty repeatedly acknowledged that under laws of war belligerents could legitimately emancipate enemy slaves. None of those demanding compensation claimed that wartime emancipation was a violation of property rights, and none revived Jefferson's charge that offering freedom to escaping slaves was an incitement to slave rebellion. Instead, the critics—following Randolph's lead—argued only that the treaty of 1783 superseded the laws of war and that Article VII

unambiguously required the British to return to their owners any slaves still on American soil when the war ended.[23]

James Madison led the opposition to the treaty and
established the limited terms on which Jay's critics would
engage the debate over compensation. He had little to say
about slavery, and what he did say was grounded in the
obligations of the treaty rather than what was permissible
under the laws of war. He complained first about the lack
of reciprocity: the British were absolved of any obligation
to pay compensation for slaves carried away in violation
of Article VII, whereas the Americans were still obliged to
pay their outstanding debts to British creditors. Madison
insinuated that the "construction" of the original treaty
Grenville offered to Jay was a recent invention, that back
in 1783 the British "uniformly admitted" that they were
obliged to compensate the Americans for any slaves they
failed to return. Carefully avoiding all discussion of how
the law of nations defined the formal legal status of the
"negroes" in question, Madison focused instead on what
he insisted were the plain, unambiguous words of Article
VII. The British claimed that under the law of nations the
slaves had been emancipated, they were no longer anyone's property, and they could not be reenslaved. Madison
answered that the positive law of the treaty prescribed the
return of slaves specified in Article VII, thereby overruling
the abstract principle of the law of nations. And even if
the United States and Great Britain had always interpreted
Article VII differently, Madison said, the proper remedy
was arbitration, not Britain's "very extraordinary abandon-
ment of the compensation due for the negroes."[24]

Critics of Jay's treaty complained that the opponents of slavery had shifted ground over the previous decade, that they were now interpreting Article VII in ways that contradicted their earlier position.[25] Had not Jay, as secretary of foreign affairs, concluded that the British owed the Americans compensation for slaves carried away in violation of the Treaty of Paris? Had not Hamilton himself sponsored a congressional resolution denouncing the British for failing to comply with Article VII? There is some truth to this accusation, but less of it than the critics imagined. Grenville may have elaborated on the British position, but it had not fundamentally changed since 1783. Hamilton claimed in 1795 that prominent legal authorities in America had always supported the British interpretation, and in the House debate a few months later some representatives claimed that they had understood all along that Article VII applied only to "the future, and could have no reference to those captured during the war and before the Treaty."[26] Nor did Jay expressly repudiate his earlier claim that the British had violated Article VII. He had suggested compensation as a solution to the impasse, but he never claimed that the Treaty of Paris required it. Jay had always doubted the moral legitimacy of Article VII and he never hid those doubts, so it was relatively easy for him to abandon the compensation claim during the 1794 negotiations.

Nevertheless, the opponents of slavery had clearly moved by 1796. They may have agreed with the British all along, but not until the debates over the Jay treaty did they formulate carefully crafted defenses of emancipation under the laws of war along with denunciations of

reenslavement as "odious." By 1795 one American statesman after another openly endorsed the position originally
taken by the British commander, Guy Carleton, at the war's
end.[27] As one congressman observed at the close of the
debate, "[I]t seems the British interpretation of the Treaty
in this respect is supported by some of our most enlightened citizens."[28] Connecticut Congressman Joshua Coit
conceded the point. Jay, Hamilton, and he himself had
only recently come to the conclusion that the British position was in fact a reasonable one, Coit explained, but this
change of heart was the product of mature deliberation on
their part. Whatever might have been John Jay's "former
opinions," Coit noted, "on attending to the subject, he had
found that what had been called the American construction was not the just one, and had therefore abandoned
it."[29] James Hillhouse, also of Connecticut, freely admitted
that a decade earlier there had been widespread criticism
of the British for violating what Americans took to be the
plain meaning of Article VII, but Hillhouse hoped that in
the intervening years tempers had cooled and a more reasonable consideration of the issue was possible.

Hillhouse presented the most thorough defense of the
antislavery position, and, like Hamilton, he started from
the premise that the language of the treaty was not clear
at all. Whenever there is disagreement over the meaning
of a treaty, Hillhouse said, the only resort of the contending parties was the law of nations. By that standard, those
demanding compensation for emancipated slaves did not
have "a well-founded claim." The first question to be asked,
Hillhouse said, was "whether negroes were to be considered

as property. There was no doubt that Article VII considered slaves as a form of property and as such contemplated the return of such property to their lawful masters. But, Hillhouse argued, a standard precept of the laws of war held that at the termination of the conflict all parties accept the condition of things on the ground at that moment. Peace could not alter those conditions. At the moment the war between England and America ended, the slaves who had come within British lines had already been emancipated. They were free, and under the laws of war the restoration of peace could not alter that fact. Article VII contemplated the return of slave "property," but there was almost no such property within British lines when the war ended. There were only freed men and women.[30] What both parties agreed to, Hillhouse concluded, was that upon acceptance of the treaty all further depredations would cease.[31]

Wherever the wording of a law or treaty was ambiguous, Hillhouse continued, "a sound rule of construction" was to decide the issue in terms "favorable to liberty" and, he wondered, "[u]nder this rule ought this Treaty to be so construed as to reduce to slavery three thousand persons who had obtained their liberty, by putting themselves under the protections of the British arms, *unless there was some positive unequivocal stipulation in the Treaty which could admit of no other construction.*"[32] Hamilton had argued that reenslavement was so palpable a violation of the principles of natural right that the British could not legitimately authorize the return of free men to slavery. By contrast, Hillhouse acknowledged the possibility that a "positive unequivocal stipulation" in a treaty could allow reenslavement. But, he asked, who could claim that Article VII rose to that standard? Who could claim that treaty called for reenslavement so clearly and unequivocally that it "could admit of no other construction"? At best Article VII was ambiguous, and by the accepted precepts of the law of nations, disputed treaties should be resolved in favor of liberty.

There was yet another principle that militated in favor of the British construction of Article VII, Hillhouse argued. If an American slave escaped to a foreign country where slavery was not legal and that country "should refuse to deliver him up," Hillhouse "very much doubted whether we should have just ground of complaint." Reiterating the argument put forward by Jay in his report to Congress a decade earlier, Hillhouse pointed out that if a white American enslaved "by one of the Barbary Powers in Africa" had escaped to Europe, "we should have good ground of complaint" if the Europeans returned the American to slavery. What difference does it make "whether the citizens of the United States are carried into slavery in Africa, or the inhabitants of Africa are brought into slavery in the United States?" Hillhouse asked. He knew of "no principle that made a difference between the natural rights of a white or a black man. The first principle that is laid down in the rights of man, is, that all men are born free and equal; it does not say all *white* men." There was no racial exception to the principle of fundamental human equality. Hillhouse would cast no aspersions on any part of the Union where slavery still existed, but neither would he question Jay's decision to act in accordance with the principles of natural law in "giving up that claim" to compensation for slaves who escaped to freedom among the British.[33]

In sharp contrast to Hillhouse's broad philosophical claims, those demanding compensation for freed slaves side-stepped nearly all discussion of the laws of war and rested their case primarily on what they claimed was the unambiguous language of Article VII.[34] No one was more heated in his denunciation of Jay and his "northern" sympathies than Congressman John Heath of Virginia. He denounced the British refusal to compensate slave owners as an "outrage against justice and morality" but he never specified which principles of "justice" and "morality" were at stake other than the fact that the British had committed a "flagrant . . . violation of the Treaty."[35] Heath's fellow Virginian, Francis Preston, was more typical of the treaty's critics. He did not dispute that under the laws of war the British became the owners of the slave property that came into their lines and were therefore within their rights to dispose of such property by emancipating the slaves. But the British had renounced their property right and with it the power to emancipate when they agreed to Article VII, which, Preston insisted, "expressly stipulated" that the slaves were to be returned to their owners. The British may not have thought the treaty obliged them to return slaves to their owners, but "[a]11 America once thought so," Preston claimed.[36]

Despite their desire to avoid the "abstract" principle of the laws of war, those demanding compensation always rested their argument on the crucial but disputed premise that the "negroes" referred to in Article VII were still *property*, and as such they had to be returned to their

owners when the war was over. Was it not, Congressman Moore asked, "an established principle amongst all
civilized nations, that plundered property shall be given
up?" Rather than counter the argument that the slaves
had already been freed, Moore simply declared that all
"negroes" within British lines were "plundered property."
Albert Gallatin did something similar in his own truncated
summation of the opposing argument. He disputed Hamilton's supposed claim that "all those who were in the hands
of the British when the Treaty of Peace was signed, must
be considered as British, and not American property." But
that isn't what Hamilton argued.

No one disputed the principle that private property
"plundered" in wartime should be returned to its rightful
owner once the war ended, so long as it was intact and
still in place. But to Jay's defenders, the African-Americans
within British lines at the moment the war ended were not
"plundered property," as Moore claimed, nor were they
"British property," as Gallatin claimed. Having been emancipated by their British owners, the blacks were no longer
property at all.[37] Connecticut Congressman Coit had earlier claimed that under "the laws of war and nations," the
slaves freed by the British "before the close of the war, had
ceased to be property of American inhabitants." Connecticut's Roger Griswold had likewise claimed that slaves "who
had fled from their masters during the war, on a promise of
emancipation . . . were no longer the property of American
inhabitants, and of course it was no violation of the Treaty
to carry them away."[38] But Coit and Griswold had framed
their argument in a way that left open the possibility that

when the war ended the slaves were *British* property, property that now had to be returned to its original American owners. This was Gallatin's point. In response, however, Congressman Uriah Tracy of Connecticut argued that if the freed people in question were not "property" but were "men," then "no law human or Divine could or ought to coerce a return to their former slavery, and no such construction could, with a shadow of propriety, be given to the words of the Treaty." Because they had been emancipated, Tracy concluded, the slaves "who had repaired to the British standard antecedent to the peace, in consequence of a proclamation promising them freedom, could by no possible construction . . . be comprehended by [Article VII] of the Treaty of Peace."[39]

None of those demanding compensation ever really addressed the argument that there was no slave property within British lines when the war ended because the slaves had already been emancipated. Instead, critics of Jay's treaty assumed that slaves not already carried away were still slaves, and insisted that the "plain sense" and "common understanding" of Article VII required the return of slave property to its previous owners.[40]

BECAUSE THERE WERE so many contentious issues raised by the Jay treaty, it is impossible to determine with any precision how the House would have voted on the issue of slave compensation alone. It's even more difficult to tell how the Senate might have voted, because its deliberations were secret. Further complicating matters is the fact that the dispute over the Jay treaty was in many ways a partisan proxy fight between Federalists and Republicans—a fight that encompassed a host of issues that had little to do with the question of whether the British owed compensation for slaves carried away after the War of Independence ended. Still, *if* the divided votes on the treaty can be read as an approximate reflection of the more specific divisions over slave compensation—admittedly a big "if"—they suggest that the majority of American statesmen in the mid-1790s believed that military emancipation was fully justified by the Enlightenment rules of war and that reenslavement was a serious violation of those same rules. The Senate endorsed the treaty by the requisite two-thirds vote and, after two months of debate, the House endorsed a resolution, "For carrying into effect the Treaty," by a 51 to 48 majority.[41] Some of the most prominent statesmen in America had urged that outcome. The treaty had been negotiated by John Jay, then chief justice of the Supreme Court, defended by Treasury Secretary Alexander Hamilton, and ratified by President George Washington.[42]

More telling was the fact that none of the critics of the treaty argued that military emancipation violated the laws of war. No one demanded the return of, or compensation for, any slaves "carried away" before the war ended. Instead, they claimed that some wartime emancipations, however legitimate, could be reversed by a treaty requiring the return of slave "property" still on American soil at the moment the war ended. Two decades after the Jay treaty, those well-established precepts shaped another debate between the British and the Americans over compensation for slaves carried away after the War of 1812 ended.

THE YEARS BETWEEN 1815 and 1828 witnessed an almost eerie replay of the debates of 1783–1796. This time the dispute centered not on Article VII of the Treaty of Paris but on the similarly worded Article I of the Treaty of Ghent. Once again, the British had offered emancipation to slaves who agreed to join the British army or navy. Once again, the British "carried away" large numbers of slaves beyond U.S. borders during the war, and both sides agreed that those slaves had been legitimately emancipated; their masters could neither demand the slaves' return nor expect compensation for them. Instead— and once again—a disagreement erupted almost immediately about the status of blacks inside British lines but still within the United States at the moment the war ended.

During the War of 1812 thousands of slaves along the Atlantic and Gulf coasts ran to British lines in response to offers of freedom in return for service in the British army or navy. Military-age men naturally responded in the greatest numbers but—as was true during the Revolution and as would also be true during the Civil War—enslaved women and children escaped on their own or alongside their husbands and fathers. By the time the War of 1812 ended, thousands of emancipated slaves had already made their way to freedom in Canada, England, and the Caribbean, but thousands more remained within British lines or were serving onboard British ships still docked in American waters. These blacks, still in American territory, became the object of dispute between Britain and America.

The British and the Americans signed the treaty at Ghent just before Christmas 1814, and disagreement quickly erupted over the precise meaning of an ambiguously worded passage. There is no doubt that the wording of Article I was convoluted, but it was also surprisingly similar to the much-debated wording of Article VII in the Treaty of Paris. The treaty specified a number of territories occupied by the British during the war that were to be evacuated "without causing any destruction or carrying away of any Artillery or other public property in the said forts or places, which shall remain therein upon the Exchange of the ratifications of this Treaty, or any Slaves or other private property."[43]

Almost immediately a familiar question resurfaced. What did the wording of the treaty mean? The most contentious issue was whether Article I treated "public" and "private" property differently. Everyone agreed that the treaty required the British to leave behind all of the "public" property that remained in the same "forts and other places" where it was originally captured and that were still occupied by the British at war's end. Public property that had already been removed to other places was not covered by the treaty. Did the same rules apply to "private property," including slaves? The British said yes—the only slaves they were required to return were those still remaining in the "forts and other places" occupied by the British during the war and explicitly "stipulated" for evacuation by the Treaty of Ghent. Not surprisingly, the Americans denounced the "extraordinary principle" that if slaves "were removed a single mile from the place of capture, they were not restorable, though still within the limits of the United States."[44] James Monroe, then the American secretary of state, dismissed Britain's "unnatural" construction of Article I and insisted that the British were obligated to return all slaves still within U.S. territory at the moment the ratifications were exchanged. If the British were right, only a handful of slaves were covered by the treaty; if the Americans were right, thousands would have to be returned.[45]

When the fighting stopped, British naval commanders along the southern Atlantic coast of the United States refused to return those men who had escaped from slavery and had been offered their freedom in return for service in his Britannic Majesty's navy. By "entering into the service," British Captain James Clavelle declared in early 1815, "they made themselves free men."[46] At first the British resisted only the return to slavery of men who were serving as sailors on their own ships. But in the ensuing months widespread British hostility to reenslavement led them to a familiar interpretation of their obligations under the law of nations. They claimed that the vast majority of slaves still on American soil who had escaped to their lines during the war were emancipated and would not be reenslaved. Article I of the Ghent treaty applied only to the small number of slaves who were still physically located within the specific "forts and other places" named in the treaty as slated for restitution. Those who had escaped from areas not occupied by the British or who had been moved elsewhere within British lines, to islands or ships on Chesapeake Bay, for example, were not covered by the treaty. Whether or not this was grammatically persuasive, it was clear that the British were relying on the sentence structure of the treaty to avoid returning thousands of men and women to slavery.

Disregarding American objections, Clavelle sailed his three ships from the Chesapeake to Bermuda with the freed slaves still on board. British Admiral Alexander Cockburn justified the action by claiming that "wherever the British flag was, there was British territory." On British territory the blacks were free men, and nothing in the treaty could possibly compel them to enslave free men serving in the British navy.[47] The dispute continued on up the British chain of command, but at every step the Americans were more rather than less frustrated. Sir Alexander Cochrane agreed only to the return of "slaves that were received in the British camp or ships *after* the ratification of the treaty." Thousands of former slaves were thereby carried away from the Chesapeake after the war ended, leaving behind only twenty-seven who met the extremely narrow British construction of their obligations under Article I of the treaty. Further south, the British acknowledged that eighty-one slaves had to be returned, but carried away sixteen hundred others. Yet so widespread was the opposition to reenslavement among ordinary British sailors that American commissioners found it difficult to enforce the already narrow interpretation of the treaty. A few of the twenty-seven slaves who had been returned to their owners quickly ran back to the British, who then informed the Americans that the runaways would be taken to Bermuda to await final determination of their status.

Still hoping to recover the slaves they believed were improperly freed, American emissaries followed the British ships to Bermuda, only to discover that most of the blacks had already gone to Halifax, Nova Scotia. When the Americans made their appeal to Bermuda's governor, Sir James

Cockburn, "he instantly lost his temper" and "vehemently" declared that "he would rather Bermuda, and every man, woman, and child in it, were sunk under the sea, than surrender one slave that had sought protection under the flag of England."[48]

The dispute that had arisen between Britain and America once again concerned slaves still on shore in the United States at the end of the war. No one expected the British to return slaves already carried away beyond U.S. borders before the war officially ended. As the American commissioners compiling a roster of slaves in British hands explained, they were charged with the recovery only of slaves "still remaining within the Chesapeake, or on the shores or islands thereof." John Quincy Adams, the U.S. ambassador to Great Britain, noted that the treaty required the British "to restore slaves taken by them from their owners in the United States during the war, and then in their possession," that is, in their possession "at the restoration of the peace." Slaves already emancipated and removed from U.S. territory before the ratifications were exchanged were not covered by the treaty, Adams agreed. "Public property" that had been removed from the places where it was captured need not be returned, Adams noted. But the slaves were private property, no different from any other form of movable private property, Adams argued, and under the terms of the treaty all private property still on American soil at war's end had to be returned to its rightful owners.[49]

The British disputed this last point. Slaves, Lord Liverpool told Adams, did not quite fit into the general category of "private property; a table or a chair, for instance, might be taken and restored without changing its condition, but a living human being was entitled to other considerations." A chair returned to its owner was still a chair. But to return a free man to his former owner was to change his condition, from person to property—a clear violation of accepted laws of war. Adams had no wish to dispute the principle. "Certainly a living, sentient being, and still more a human being, was to be regarded in a different light from the inanimate matter of which other private property might consist." But having conceded the salience of Liverpool's point, Adams fell back on the standard American position: treaty obligations trump the abstract principles of natural right; this treaty clearly defined the "negroes" still on shore as private property. If the British had objections, they should have raised them during the negotiations, but having signed the treaty it was too late to make the claim.[50]

Not surprisingly, the broad principles invoked by the British to justify emancipation were reduced by the Americans to squabbles over the precise wording of the treaty. And as usual the Americans claimed that the wording of the treaty was clear and unambiguous. But this time the British answered with a detailed analysis of Article I, contradicting the American reading word by word and comma by comma. First, Lord Bathurst spelled out the British interpretation, then Lord Castlereagh sustained Bathurst. His Majesty's government, Castlereagh wrote to Adams on April 10, 1816, "deny that the United States can have any claim to property not actually in the places which, by the stipulations of the treaty, were to be restored at the time specified therein." The Americans complained that the British were resorting to petty rules of grammar to get around the plain sense of the treaty, and too many American historians have casually repeated the accusation. But for more than thirty years the British had been insisting that they would never have agreed to a treaty requiring the reenslavement of the men and women who had escaped to British lines during wartime having been promised their freedom. Reduced to a dispute over sentence structure, the British position can easily be made to seem unreasonable. But within the context of long-standing British policy, Castlereagh's position was perfectly consistent. Under his reading of Article I of the Ghent treaty, the British had every right to evacuate most of the blacks "on shore" because most of them had been emancipated "previous to the ratification of the treaty."[51]

Adams disputed much more than the British reading of the treaty. He also claimed that under the laws of war the British had no right to "seduce" *any* slaves from their masters at *any* point during the war. It was true that the treaty required the return only of those slaves still on American soil when the war ended, Adams noted, but this was a concession to the British. Our goal in the negotiations, he insisted to Lord Liverpool, "was to secure the restoration of both public and private property, including slaves, which had in any manner been captured on shore during the war." He described the seduction and removal of slaves as "deviations from the usages of war." As "private property," the slaves "ought never to have been taken" to begin with. What did Adams mean by this? He appears to be saying something new to the history of American diplomacy: that "private property" in slaves can "never" be taken under the "usages of war."[52]

This was the single most extreme argument against military emancipation made by any American statesman before the Civil War. In the late eighteenth century, during all the years of dispute over the Treaty of Paris and the Jay treaty, not even the most ardent American critics of the British had claimed that freeing slaves in wartime was a violation of the laws of war. On the contrary, most of the American leaders demanding compensation had freely conceded the right of belligerents to entice slaves with offers of freedom in wartime. They claimed instead that the treaty ending the War of Independence overrode some, though not all, of the wartime emancipations. Coming twenty years later, Adams's wholesale denunciation of military emancipation may reflect the emergence of a more militant proslavery argument. It may reflect the increasing influence of slaveholders in national politics. Or it may have been sui generis. It's hard to find anyone else talking the way Adams was talking in 1816. Despite Adams's claim that the laws of war did not sanction the emancipation of enemy slaves, no American official—neither President James Madison, Secretary of State James Monroe, nor Adams himself—appears to have demanded the return of, or compensation for, slaves already freed and carried beyond the borders of the United States during the War of 1812.

British officials held out the possibility that their offers of freedom to one specific group did violate the terms of the treaty—those slaves in Louisiana and Georgia who had taken refuge within British fortifications at the end of the war.[53] Andrew Jackson's famous victory over the British at New Orleans had taken place after the fighting on the

Atlantic coast had come to an end and the two sides had begun peace negotiations. As a result, at the moment the treaty was signed, a number of slaves in the Deep South were still residing in the places to which they had originally escaped. British commanders in those areas still refused to return those people to slavery and instead transported them to freedom in the usual places—Nova Scotia, the Bahamas, or as far away as England, and those removals, the British agreed, did violate the terms of the treaty. Because British officials opposed reenslavement, they would only agree to compensate the Americans for slaves freed in Georgia and Louisiana at the very end of the war.

Here, then, was the point of dispute that dragged on for several years after the Treaty of Ghent had been signed. The Americans demanded the return of all slaves still "on shore" when the ratifications were exchanged, and if the British refused to return them, the Americans wanted compensation instead. Those still on shore included two large groups—the thousands of slaves from Maryland and Virginia who had escaped to the British during the war but who were transported to permanent freedom only after the war ended, as well as those slaves in Louisiana and Georgia who were still residing in British fortifications when the ratifications were exchanged. The British refused to return all but a handful of slaves and were willing to compensate the Americans only for those slaves still residing in the specific places that the treaty stipulated were to be returned to the United States. This meant that they would neither return nor pay compensation for the thousands of former slaves removed from the Chesapeake after the war ended.

In 1818 the United States and Britain agreed to allow the czar of Russia to arbitrate the dispute, but it was several years before the arbitration proceedings were concluded. Even the czar himself recognized that the contest was, at bottom, a "grammatical question" about the meaning of Article I of the Ghent treaty—that is, "the signification of the words in the text of the article as it now is." Did the wording of the treaty require the British to return all slaves "on shore" at war's end—as the Americans maintained—or the much smaller number of slaves residing in the "forts and other places" stipulated for restitution?

On July 12, 1822, Czar Alexander I issued his decision, resoundingly endorsing the British reading of the treaty. The United States was entitled to "a just indemnification" only for those slaves "carried away from places and territories of which the Treaty stipulates the restitution." As for the thousands of slaves carried away from areas "not stipulated" for restitution—all the slaves "on shore," in Adams's words—the czar ruled, "the United States are *not* entitled to claim an indemnification for the said slaves." As the emperor went on to explain, Article I did distinguish between public and private property, but "these two prohibitions are solely applicable to the places of which the article stipulates the restitution."[54] This had been the British position all along— the prohibition on the removal of private property, including slaves, applied only to slaves physically located in those places specifically slated for restitution in the treaty.

Not surprisingly, the British read the czar's decision as a vindication. By virtue of the ruling, Sir Charles Bagot declared, "his Britannic Majesty is not bound to indemnify the United States for any slaves who, coming from places which have never been occupied by his troops, voluntarily joined the British forces, either in consequence of the encouragement which his Majesty's officers had offered to them, or to free themselves from the power of their master." The Americans were not entitled by the treaty to any compensation for such slaves, Bagot explained, "not having been carried away from places of which the article stipulated the restitution." The Russian emperor concurred. When pressed by the Americans for further elaboration, Alexander I reaffirmed his conclusion that compensation was due to the Americans only for slaves carried away from areas stipulated for restitution in the treaty. This, the Russians acknowledged, was "also the sense which Sir Charles Bagot attached" to the decision.[55]

But the Americans acted as though the emperor had ruled in their favor and proceeded to draw up elaborate lists of slaves carried away from places not specified for restitution in the treaty. The Americans further demanded that the British pay hundreds of thousands of dollars in interest payments on the slaves carried away ten years earlier. When the Americans presented these demands to the commission charged with implementing the arbitration ruling, the British commissioner balked. He demanded proof that the claims for slaves were valid and flatly rejected the demand for interest payments. The Americans were infuriated by the British refusal to cooperate, and the entire commission process broke down. Finally the secretary of state, Henry Clay, sent Albert Gallatin to London to negotiate a compromise. Gallatin had been an outspoken critic of the Jay treaty, and from London sent home remarkable letters boasting about the tongue-lashings he administered to the British for their supposed violation, decades earlier, of the Treaty of Paris. The British, no doubt disgusted by American impertinence, finally agreed to pay a flat amount—£250,000—to fulfill any and all obligations arising from the Russian arbitration. The disagreement over what those obligations were was thus rendered moot, for the British had effectively washed their hands of the matter by leaving it entirely up to the Americans to decide how and to whom the funds would be disbursed.[56]

Gallatin's diplomacy is generally seen as a victory for the Americans. Had they not, after all, won the compensation they had always claimed was their due? But the Americans did not want compensation when the war ended; they wanted their slaves back, and they never got them. The British in turn had always been willing to compensate the Americans for slaves freed in violation of the Ghent treaty. The dispute arose from the fact that Americans demanded compensation for many more slaves than the British were willing to concede had been improperly removed. Whether the final payment was a victory for the Americans or the British is at least open to debate. Consider the amount of compensation the British paid. In the wake of the arbitration decision, the U.S. commissioners had compiled a "definitive list" of the slaves and other property carried off by the British, property the Americans valued at $2,693,120. In the end, however, the British government paid less than half of what the Americans had asked for, a total of $1,204,960 for the "slaves and other property carried away in contravention of the treaty of Ghent."[57] As far as the British were concerned, they were compensating the Americans only for slaves carried off from the precise areas stipulated in the Ghent treaty and affirmed by the Russian arbitration. The Americans, of course, never accepted that narrow interpretation of either the treaty or the czar's decision, and the lump-sum payment persuaded them that they had won the point, for they were free to distribute the money as they saw fit. It turned out that the British avoided a miserable headache.

As soon as American officials assumed control of the distribution of the compensation funds, they were bedeviled by an unseemly squabble among slaveholders competing for the money. The problem arose because masters in states invaded early in the war—Maryland and Virginia in particular—were entitled to very little compensation: most of their slaves were carried away before the war ended. Slave owners in states invaded relatively late in the war—Georgia and Louisiana, for example—would end up getting most of the money. As Secretary of State Henry Clay explained in 1825, of the twenty-four hundred slaves "carried away" from Virginia and Maryland, "not more than five hundred will probably be brought, by the proof, within the terms of the treaty of Ghent." In the first round of distribution masters from Georgia and Louisiana got most of the money because "all these are supposed to be comprehended by the provision of the treaty."[58] The quarrel erupted over what was left.

Masters from Maryland and Virginia demanded a share of the remaining funds even though they were unable to document their claims. Slave owners from Georgia and Louisiana wanted most of the remaining money for themselves, even though they had already gotten the bulk of the original fund. Chesapeake slaveholders claimed that their proofs were lost when the British burned their homes, but Louisianans insinuated that the Chesapeake claimants were lying and insisted that that they produce documentation. The agent for the Chesapeake slaveholders denounced the "ungracious and selfish" behavior of the Deep South masters and, in one extraordinary move, he threatened to revive the British argument against compensating masters for slaves carried away from Dauphin Island because the island was technically Spanish territory at the moment the war ended.[59] Attorney General William Wirt, arguing as a private attorney for the Chesapeake claimants, urged the commission distributing the leftover funds to presume postwar removal unless someone came forth with specific evidence to the contrary. The commission agreed, and the Chesapeake slaveholders ended up getting a share of the remaining compensation funds, thanks to the legal fiction that most of their slaves had been carried away after the war was over.[60]

By fighting among themselves over whether their slaves had been emancipated *after* the war, the slaveholders implicitly affirmed the long-standing American principle that slaves freed *during* the war were gone forever, without compensation. Nobody denied this but, curiously, nobody said it either. Unlike the Jay treaty debate, neither the British nor the Americans spent much time arguing about what was permissible under the general rules of civilized warfare. Adams had said that the postwar removal of slaves violated the "usages of war," and the British occasionally tweaked the Americans for claiming that slaves were indistinguishable from chairs or horses. But mostly the compensation debate centered on precisely what the Treaty of Ghent did or did not require. As Czar Alexander noted, the dispute between Britain and the United States rested almost entirely on "the interpretation of the first article of the treaty." Both sides "have appealed only as a subsidiary means to the general principles of the law of nations."[61] But this in itself was telling. Americans continued to accept that slaves freed under the laws of war and "removed" from the United States during the war were beyond recovery, but they also insisted that the final status of "negroes or other property" still "on shore" at war's end was determined not by the general principles of the laws of war, but by the requirements of the treaty that ended the war. The positive law of a treaty still trumped the abstract rules of war, and until the 1830s this was a premise that appealed to slaveholders demanding compensation. But when war erupted between the United States and the Seminole Indians in Florida in December 1835, it was the opponents of slavery who insisted on the superior force of treaties.

THE LONGEST OF all the "Indian wars" of the nineteenth century, the conflict with the Seminoles was also—as the U.S. commander in charge of the operation explained—"a negro war."[62] Hundreds of slaves had escaped into Florida from the neighboring southern states. Thousands more blacks were working on plantations owned by whites, concentrated in the area around St. Augustine. Still others were enslaved to the Seminoles. When the war broke out in December 1835, it proved impossible to keep slavery out of it. The free blacks, having escaped from southern slavery, naturally allied with the Seminoles, with whom they often shared close ties of community and kinship. Seminole leaders made concerted and successful efforts to entice the slaves of white planters with offers of freedom in return for military service.

U.S. Major General Thomas Jesup, in command of the American forces, tried repeatedly to coerce the Seminoles into a surrender followed by their removal to the West, to no avail. The sticking point was slavery: Jesup wanted the Indians to hand over their "allies," the free blacks living in Florida having escaped from slavery in the South. The Seminoles refused until, at last, Jesup yielded to their demand. The fifth article of capitulation stipulated that "[t]he Seminoles and their allies, who come in and emigrate West, shall be secure in their lives and property." As the antislavery Congressman Joshua Giddings explained, the "language of this article could not be misunderstood." The blacks who were living among the Indians, "acting with them, and fighting our troops, were their '*allies*.'"[63]

For Giddings, writing in 1858, the lesson was obvious. In offering slaves freedom during wartime, Jesup was following long-established precedents set by the British and the Americans in both the War of Independence and the War of 1812. "It is a principle understood by all intelligent men," Giddings concluded, "that when war exists, peace may be obtained by the emancipation of all the slaves held by individuals, if necessary."[64] Jesup's promise of emancipation, then, was fully in accord with the familiar principles of military emancipation. Naturally, Giddings thought it reprehensible that General Jesup reversed his decision after the slaveholders brought intense pressure to bear on Secretary

of War Lewis Cass. Backing away from his original promise, Jesup rushed into a second agreement, this time with an
"unimportant chief," requiring the Seminoles to "surrender
the negroes of white men, particularly those taken during
the war." Jesup's original guarantee of emancipation was
consistent with accepted American standards of conduct in
wartime, Giddings wrote. The second agreement, however,
was a "violation of the solemn articles of capitulation, which
these officers termed a *treaty,* and which certainly possessed
all the solemnity and binding force of a treaty."[65] A treaty was
a treaty, Giddings insisted, and the one Jesup had negotiated had guaranteed the freedom of the former slaves who
escaped to live among the Seminoles—whether before or
during the war.

Jesup's capitulation to the slaveholders backfired. By
betraying his promise to respect the freedom of the former
slaves, he plunged Florida back into war. Blacks in the state
were no longer fighting against removal to the West; they
were fighting to preserve their own freedom. Desperate to
separate the highly motivated blacks from their Seminole
allies, American military commanders renewed the promise
of liberty and offered to respect the freedom of any former
slaves who surrendered on their own. This offer stuck. Slaveholders in Georgia and Florida vehemently protested all the
way to the floor of Congress. When Zachary Taylor took
command of the Florida operations, he refused to renege
on the promise of freedom. In one engagement, in 1838,
Taylor captured a number of fugitive slaves, but when their
owners arrived at camp Taylor would not reenslave them, on
the grounds that they were prisoners of war. They had been

promised their freedom, and by the well-known rules of civilized warfare—especially as enunciated by Vattel—prisoners of war could not be enslaved. Taylor reported his decision to the War Department, it was approved, and the black prisoners were sent west as free men.

The same thing happened in New Orleans where, in 1838, owners made another attempt to claim the westbound slaves by sending the sheriff to the army camp to collect them. But the commander of the military district, General Edmund P. Gaines, turned the sheriff away and ended up in court defending his action. The blacks were prisoners of war, Gaines argued, and "he could recognize no other power in time of war, or by the laws of war, as authorized to take prisoners from his possession." He also claimed that military emancipation could free far more than fighting-age men. In time of war ordinary slave workers were "belligerents as much as their masters" because their labor was used to sustain enemy forces in the field. Slave men cultivated the earth; slave women cooked the food, nursed the sick, and thereby "contribute to the maintenance of the war." Even the labor of children was impressed into service to sustain the war. Hence the army was within its authority, under the laws of war, to emancipate all enemy slaves—men, women, and children alike. Finally, Gaines argued, military officers lacked the judicial authority to determine anyone's formal legal status. When the sheriff arrived at his camp demanding the return of those claimed as slaves, he was asking soldiers to assume a judicial authority that soldiers did not have. The state laws of Florida were irrelevant, Gaines claimed. Soldiers could only "be guided by the laws of war, and whatever may be the laws of any State, they must yield to the safety of the federal government." Gaines, like Taylor, sent the slaves west as free people.[66]

During the Seminole War, then, U.S. officials—including army officers on the ground, a succession of American presidents, and even Congress—sustained the military emancipation of hundreds of escaped and captured slaves over the strenuous protests of their former owners. In the process, the federal government established a number of precedents that would later be invoked by Union officials during the Civil War as justification for military emancipation. The Lincoln administration insisted that it was illegal under the laws of war to enslave a prisoner of war, even if the prisoner was an escaped slave. A few months after the Civil War started, Union officials endorsed the principle that slave women and children could be "confiscated" from their owners and emancipated because their labor was indispensable to the enemy's ability to sustain the war. By late 1861 Republicans in Congress were insisting that if a sheriff or a master showed up at a military camp demanding the return of a slave, soldiers could not comply with the demand because they lacked the judicial authority to do so. The military was guided only by the laws of war, and those laws neither recognized slavery nor sanctioned reenslavement.

The precedents established during the Florida conflict exposed the emancipatory potential of the laws of war, and no one recognized this more clearly—or more ironically—than John Quincy Adams. Beginning in 1836, shortly after the Seminole War broke out, Adams began making a series of extraordinary claims about the federal government's authority to free slaves under the war and treaty-making powers sanctioned by the Constitution. The claims were astonishing in part because of their novelty and in part because of who was making them.

Between 1815 and 1828—as secretary of state, as the American ambassador to Britain, and as president—Adams had been the most extreme defender of U.S. claims for compensation. Indeed, no American statesman had ever argued so strenuously that military emancipation was a "deviation" from the laws of war. After he left the presidency in 1829, Adams returned to Washington as a congressman from Massachusetts and there, in the House of Representatives, he argued that the Constitution vested Congress with the power to emancipate American slaves if necessary to suppress a domestic insurrection. This looked to many like a scandalous reversal of his earlier position.

On May 25, 1836, Adams denounced as "false and utterly untrue" a seemingly uncontroversial resolution that declared: "Congress possesses no constitutional authority to interfere in any way with the institution of slavery in any of the States of this Confederacy." That the resolution affirmed nothing more than the federal consensus, shared by radical abolitionists and proslavery reactionaries alike, was revealed in the final vote endorsing it, 182 yeas to 9 nays.[67] Yet Adams voted against the resolution, and he justified his vote by citing the recent dispute with Great Britain over Article I of the Treaty of Ghent. During the war British military commanders had enticed large numbers of slaves to their standard with promises of freedom, Adams noted. But "by the treaty of peace, Great Britain stipulated to evacuate all forts and places in the United States, without carrying away any slaves." In effect the Treaty of Ghent required the federal government to "interfere" with slavery in the southern states to protect it against British depredations. If the federal government had no power to interfere with slavery in the southern states, Adams argued, it could never have negotiated such a stipulation. Treaties were powerful legal instruments, he noted. They could reenslave people who had freed themselves during the war, but they could also emancipate slaves within the southern states, and either way there was nothing the state could do about it.[68]

Adams's speech justifying federal interference with slavery was prompted by a bill to relieve the suffering of those left desperate by the Florida war. According to Adams, there was nothing in the constitutional powers of the government that could justify federal expenditures on behalf of suffering individuals during peacetime. The appropriation could only be based on the war powers—powers not specified in the Constitution and "limited and regulated only by the laws and usages of nations." For the same reason, and under similar circumstances, the U.S. government would be within its powers to free slaves in the southern states.[69] The Seminole War proved the point. General Jesup had labeled it "a negro war," and Adams concurred. This was a "servile war," he said, "complicated" by an Indian war. Now "suppose Congress were called to raise armies, to supply money from the whole Union to suppress a servile insurrection, would they have no authority to interfere with the institution of slavery?" During a war, Adams explained, "the slave may emancipate himself." The slaveholder in turn may be compelled "to recognize his emancipation by a treaty of peace."

Wasn't the federal government empowered to negotiate such a treaty? Adams asked. Can it be said "that Congress, in such a contingency, would have no authority to interfere with the institution of slavery, *in any way*, in the States? Why, it would be equivalent to saying that Congress have no constitutional authority to make peace."[70] The power to make war was inseparable from the power to make peace.

Adams then launched into a savage denunciation of American attempts to provoke a war with Mexico in hopes of restoring slavery to Texas. A war like that, once begun, could scarcely be contained, Adams warned. He conjured up images of global conflagration, with European powers rushing into the fray—in Britain's case to protect its recent abolition of slavery in the West Indies and, in the cases of France and Spain, to protect slavery in their own colonies. Indian nations would rise up en masse. Mexico would fight to the death to protect itself from the aggressive march of southern slaveholders. The slaves themselves would rise up in rebellion, emancipating themselves, transforming the war into a "great conflict" between "slavery and emancipation." In such circumstances as these, Adams asked—dramatically repeating his earlier question—"Do you imagine that your Congress will have no constitutional authority to interfere with the institution of slavery *in any way* in the States of this Confederacy?" His own answer was unequivocal. One way or another, Congress would interfere with slavery, whether to "sustain it by war" or "perhaps to abolish it by treaties of peace."[71]

Adams had done a couple of remarkable things. He took an utterly conventional proposition—that slaves could be emancipated in wartime but that treaties determined the ultimate fate of emancipated slaves—and turned it into a revolutionary new argument that the federal government could actually *abolish* slavery in a state by means of a treaty. He would not therefore endorse congressional resolutions reaffirming the conventional wisdom that Congress could not interfere with slavery in the states. It looked as if Adams had moved, literally, from one extreme to the other. His 1816 claim that the laws of war did not sanction the emancipation of enemy slaves appears to have been far more aggressive than that of any other American statesmen at the time. His 1836 claim that the treaty powers of the Constitution allowed the federal government to abolish slavery in a southern state was no less extraordinary.

But the two positions, though equally extreme, were not necessarily inconsistent. In 1816 Adams claimed that a belligerent could not emancipate enemy slaves under the laws of war. But in 1836 he said that slaves could take advantage of a war to emancipate themselves—which was not quite the same thing. Suspicious of arguments grounded solely in natural law, Adams had earlier dismissed the right of belligerents to free enemy slaves under the abstract, unwritten laws of war. Twenty years later, he was defending the right of the federal government to emancipate American slaves— not enemy slaves—and his source for that authority was not the abstract laws of war but the war-powers clause of the Constitution backed up by positive congressional statute. In short, Adams was talking about two different situations and, arguably, two different bodies of law. He was most consistent in claiming that the final status of the slaves was determined by a treaty. Even in 1836 he was still citing Ghent as evidence that a treaty could compel the return of slave property, but he was drawing a very different lesson. If a treaty could require reenslavement, it could just as easily require abolition. Thus from arguably identical precepts Adams came to seemingly antithetical conclusions. He had reversed the polarity of his argument, but it was still the same argument.

Not even the most radical antislavery congressmen were willing to go quite as far as Adams. On March 21, 1842, Giddings introduced a series of resolutions designed to show that slaves who rebelled on the high seas were freed because they were outside the jurisdiction of the "municipal" laws of the states, which alone could enslave them. Under the Articles of Confederation power over slavery resided exclusively with the states, Giddings noted, and with the adoption of the Constitution "no part of the aforesaid powers were delegated to the Federal Government."[72] This was the familiar peacetime prohibition on federal interference with slavery in the states. But notwithstanding his own close relationship to Giddings, Adams once again objected to the resolution on the grounds that the war and treaty-making powers nullified the prohibition. Giddings, in fact, did not dispute Adams on the point. In his 1858 book on the Seminole War, Giddings upheld the federal government's power to emancipate slaves in wartime and to protect those emancipations by means of a treaty.

But for Giddings and most antislavery politicians— including radicals like Charles Sumner and Thaddeus Stevens—the war powers were incidental to their goal of destroying slavery. They continued to press for a peacetime program of abolition achieved by the deliberate encirclement of the slave states within a cordon of freedom. And so, unlike Adams, they continued to affirm the consensus against federal interference with slavery in the states. They were not contemplating war. But neither did antislavery radicals repudiate military emancipation. Why would they? Military emancipation was a mainstream practice, whether sanctioned by the unwritten laws of war or by the war powers clause of the Constitution. John Quincy Adams never denied that slaves could "emancipate themselves" in wartime. It should hardly surprise us, then, that during the secession winter of 1860/61, threats of military emancipation sprang up everywhere in the Republican speeches and editorials. So ordinary was the theory and practice of freeing slaves in wartime that it would have been surprising had Republicans *not* raised the threat as soon as it looked like there would be war.

LIKE THE BRITISH during the War of Independence, Union officials in 1861 began by offering emancipation to rebel-owned slaves who emancipated themselves by coming within their lines. Service in the Union army—like service in the British or the Continental armies—was considered a guarantee of emancipation. In the 1790s leading American statesmen argued that when slaves escaped to the enemy in wartime, the property right was transferred and the new owner was within his rights to emancipate the slaves. In June 1861, Benjamin Butler was saying the same thing about the "contraband" slaves coming within his line in Virginia. We know that the slaves were "property" under the laws of the states from which they escaped, Butler wrote, but "we do not need and will not hold such property."[73] One month later Congress and the Lincoln administration declared that "persons held to service" who escaped to Union lines from disloyal states were thereafter "discharged" from service—emancipated.

From the earliest months of the Civil War the precedents set during the Seminole War echoed loudly among Union generals, administration officials, and Republican policy makers. Slaves who come within our lines can never be returned to slavery, Lincoln said in July 1861. Military commanders argued that slaves whose labor sustained the confederate war effort—not only men, but women and children as well—or who provided assistance to the Union army, could be legitimately freed under the laws of war. Republicans in Congress declared that Union soldiers of whatever rank lacked the judicial authority to determine anyone's legal status and therefore had no power to turn blacks over to masters or sheriffs who showed up demanding the return of their slaves.

Like the Americans of the founding generation, Lincoln and his fellow Republicans were always conscious of the distinction between slaves who had been "practically" emancipated—that is, physically removed from the control of their owners—and those who were still in place on their owners' farms and plantations at the moment the war ended. Military emancipation was legitimate under the laws of war, but when peace was restored so was the positive law of slavery in the southern states. Until the ratification of the Thirteenth Amendment or the abolition of slavery by the states themselves, the threat of reenslavement hung over millions of southern blacks technically embraced by the Emancipation

Proclamation but not actually—"practically" was Lincoln's word—emancipated. Yet reenslavement always had the taint of illegitimacy about it. Jay had questioned the morality of reenslavement in 1786. Hamilton called reenslavement an "infamous" violation of the laws of war. To return to slavery those who had been promised their freedom, Sir Guy Carleton had told General Washington, would be a "dishonorable Violation of the public faith." Eighty years later Abraham Lincoln said that to allow reenslavement would be "a cruel and an astounding breach of faith."[74]

Not surprisingly, the Lincoln administration's most rigorous justification of military emancipation rehearsed the familiar antislavery premises of the Enlightenment. Drafted by the distinguished law professor Francis Lieber, and published as General Orders No. 100 in April 1863, military emancipation was incorporated for the first time into the code of conduct that was supposed to govern the operations of the Union army. According to Lieber's code, slavery had no place in the laws of nature, upon which the laws of war are based. "[S]o far as the laws of nature are concerned," Lieber wrote, "all men are equal." Slavery "exists according to municipal or local law only," but those positive laws are suspended in wartime, overridden by the laws of war. So whenever the United States goes to war with "a belligerent which admits of slavery," Lieber argued, any runaway who escapes into the lines of the U.S. military "is immediately entitled to the rights and privileges of a freeman."[75] Lieber's defense of military emancipation was utterly unoriginal. It harkened back to Blackstone and Montesquieu and Somerset—the principles proclaimed by the British and openly acknowledged by virtually all American statesmen in the aftermath of the American Revolution.

Given the way military emancipation was implemented and justified, it's hard not to conclude that Republican policy makers were intimately acquainted with the precedents for freeing slaves in wartime and the principles upon which it was based. But the very familiarity, the ordinariness, of what Union officials were doing is misleading because they ended up doing something very unusual. They began by freeing some slaves in order to suppress the rebellion; they eventually used military emancipation to destroy slavery altogether. It was common to free enemy slaves in wartime to undermine a rebellion or win a war. But to deploy military emancipation as a means of destroying slavery was nothing short of revolutionary.

What was new to the Civil War was *universal* military emancipation. The number of blacks freed by the British during the War of Independence barely amounted to 5 percent of the slave population. Lord Dunmore was trying to undermine the American rebellion, not abolish slavery. The same was true of the slave liberations during the War of 1812—no matter how principled the British were in their refusal to reenslave blacks, they were not trying to abolish slavery. The precedents established during the Seminole War were far more important than the number of slaves freed—only a few hundred. The Civil War was different. Although the earliest emancipations, accomplished under the terms of the First Confiscation Act, were limited in ways that reflected well-established precedents, they were also intended by Republican policy makers to undermine the institution of slavery along with the southern rebellion. By the middle of 1862 the Union was explicitly committed to an unprecedented policy of universal military emancipation. Rather than free hundreds or thousands of slaves, they were aiming to free millions.

As northern officials pushed the familiar practice of military emancipation toward a new and revolutionary extreme, southern leaders responded by moving in the opposite direction, toward an equally extreme denunciation of the very idea of freeing slaves in wartime. Confederate officials, led by Jefferson Davis, routinely condemned military emancipation as "barbaric," a violation of all known rules of warfare among civilized peoples. To be sure, there had long been voices— southern and northern alike—equating the enticement of slaves into enemy lines with incitement to servile insurrection. Even Hamilton, in his vigorous defense of the lawfulness of military emancipation, labeled the practice "illiberal" and "infamous." But those voices were muted by the fact that Americans themselves engaged in the practice, and by the countervailing conviction that—however infamous—military emancipation was fully justified by the enlightened rules of civilized warfare. This was the conviction that, throughout the Civil War, Confederate leaders routinely denied.

Emancipation sent Davis into spasms of outrage. He called the Yankees devils and likened them to animals. Freeing people was a war crime, he thought—the moral equivalent of burning cities to the ground. The Emancipation Proclamation rendered him apoplectic. "Every crime which could characterize the course of demons has marked the course of the invader," he declared a few days into 1863. A "brutal soldiery" has swarmed into the South, "your towns to sack, your homes to pillage and incite servile insurrection." Emancipation "so utterly disgraced" the Union war effort, Davis told an audience in Richmond, Virginia, that "if the question was proposed to you whether you would combine with hyenas or Yankees, I trust every Virginian would say, Give me hyenas."[76] A week later, in rhetoric only slightly more temperate, Davis once again denounced the Emancipation Proclamation as "the most execrable measure recorded in the history of guilty man." Millions of human beings "of an inferior race" were now "doomed to extinction, while at the same time they are excited to a general assassination of their masters." Northern soldiers captured while attempting to enforce the Emancipation Proclamation would be treated, Davis vowed, like "criminals engaged in exciting servile insurrection."[77]

Two months after Lieber's code of war justifying military emancipation was published as General Orders No. 100, John Seddon, the Confederate secretary of war, produced a detailed response. It was an incoherent document, Seddon charged, two-faced, in fact. It simultaneously reaffirmed and repudiated the military restraint that was the central precept of the laws of war. Lieber had cloaked savagery with the rhetoric of civilization. The Confederate states, Seddon claimed, adhered to the known rules of civilized warfare not only in theory, but in practice. They agreed, for example, that martial law should be "strictly guided by the principles of justice, honor, and humanity." They likewise agreed "that it is a violation of the laws of war and the principles of humanity to murder, enslave, or carry off to distant parts private citizens." But although both sides claimed to be guided by principles of "justice," and both disavowed enslavement or carrying off of "private citizens," Seddon insisted, only the Confederacy abided by these principles. Under the "imperious" doctrine of "military necessity," he argued, the Union army has abandoned "justice and right."[78]

At the heart of Seddon's complaint about the Lieber code was a fundamental dispute over the status of slaves and slavery under the laws of war. Where Lieber claimed that the emancipation of enemy slaves was recognized under the laws of war, Seddon denied it. The North's official policy of enticing slaves to escape to Union lines amounted, in Seddon's view, to "the employment of servile insurrection as an instrument of war" and was "contrary to the usages of civilized nations." To prove his point, Seddon recited a highly selective version of American history from which all traces of antislavery were systematically erased. Where Lieber claimed that slavery was not recognized under the law of nations, Seddon argued that the U.S. Supreme Court "has determined that slavery and the slave trade are not contrary to the law of nations." Seddon likewise pointed to the correspondence of American diplomats and the "solemn treaties" signed by the United States and requiring "reclamations for the value of escaping slaves and of slaves abducted by a military force." Foreign nations recognized these claims, according to Seddon. Consequently, the passages in Lieber's code on the subject of slavery were "a specimen of pedantic impertinence without a parallel."[79]

Seddon offered a few specific examples of Union "impertinence," the most troubling of which was "the enlistment of negro slaves as part of the army of the United States."

The only possible reason the North could have for arming black slaves was to "subvert by violence the social system" of the South, thereby adding the "calamities of war" to the horrors of "servile insurrection." By such means, "[t]he savage passions and brutal appetites of a barbarous race are to be stimulated into fierce activity." In embarking on its policy of black recruitment, Seddon argued, the Union had "necessarily" abandoned all the "rules, conventions, mitigating influences, and humanizing usages" of the laws of war. Stripped of the rhetoric and the racism, Seddon's point had some validity. By the middle of 1862 Republican policy makers had decided to use military emancipation in an entirely new way, to "subvert by violence the social system" of the South.

When Seddon claimed that the Confederates would never enslave prisoners of war, he discerned no inconsistency with his own government's policy of reenslaving black Union soldiers. Rather, Seddon was assuming that Union emancipation had no legal legitimacy in the southern states. Here the conflict over the laws of war was starkly exposed—with disastrous consequences. By systematically reenslaving Union soldiers who had been slaves before the war, the Confederate government forced the Lincoln administration to make a painful choice. Either the Union could ignore the moral taint that had always attached to reenslavement and instead allow its own black soldiers to be reenslaved, or it could insist that formerly enslaved black soldiers be treated as legitimate prisoners of war with all the familiar safeguards that attached to the condition. There was no middle ground. Either claiming black people as private property was a just and reasonable practice and the Confederates therefore had every right to reenslave soldiers freed by the Union, or emancipation was itself "an act of justice" and the Union had every right to demand that their black men in uniform be recognized and treated as proper prisoners of war. Unwilling to accede to proslavery morality, the Lincoln administration halted prisoner exchanges in hopes of forcing the Confederates to stop enslaving black Union soldiers. Unwilling to accede to antislavery morality, the Confederates allowed prisoner-of-war camps to swell beyond their ability to care for the inmates. As a result of the stalemate tens of thousands of northern and southern soldiers perished in filthy, overcrowded, and disease-ridden prisoner-of-war camps during the Civil War.[80]

Northerners and Southerners regularly accused each other of atrocious violations of the laws of civilized warfare. In practice, it's hard to tell the two sides apart. For all their stated devotion to the sanctity of private property, Confederate officials systematically destroyed their own citizens' cotton and impressed their slaves as a "military necessity." Months before Sherman torched Atlanta, Confederate troops invaded Pennsylvania and burned Chambersburg to the ground. Both northern and southern armies foraged for supplies from the countryside. But only the Yankees freed slaves, and only the Confederates reenslaved them.

Ironically, the most conspicuous departure from the widely accepted principle of military emancipation was the Confederacy's suicidal refusal to offer freedom to some of its slaves in return for military service in defense of southern independence. There were a million adult men enslaved in the southern states in 1860. Had the Confederates enlisted 250,000 of them—a mere 6 percent of the slave population—in return for freedom and colonization, the balance of military power might have shifted decisively in favor of the South. If both sides employed black soldiers, prisoner exchanges might not have been halted and the calamity of Civil War prison camps might have been avoided. It would not have been unusual for the Confederacy to free some of its slaves in order to preserve slavery itself. Historical precedent and abstract principle would have supported the policy. Yet by the very nature of what the Confederacy was, it deprived itself of the most potent weapon at its disposal—an army of slaves fighting for their own liberation.

Abraham Lincoln grasped the novelty of the situation in a remarkable resolution he drafted in April 1863. Throughout human history, he noted, "States and Nations have tolerated slavery." But only recently, for the first time in the history of the world, "an attempt has been made to construct a new Nation, upon the basis of, and with the primary, and fundamental object to maintain, enlarge, and perpetuate human slavery."[81] To protect and preserve the ancient practice of human slavery, the Confederacy was forced to repudiate the equally ancient practice of arming slaves, and with it the enlightened justification of military emancipation. The irreconcilable conflict over slavery had become an irreconcilable conflict over the laws of war.

EPILOGUE:

Harriet Beecher Stowe and Her British Sisters

I T WAS NOVEMBER 1862 and Harriet Beecher Stowe was frustrated. Not with the progress of the Union war effort, or with President Lincoln's supposedly slow path to emancipation, but with the failure of the British to understand what was going on in the United States. They were misreading Lincoln's speeches. The Republican Party confused them. They didn't grasp the Constitution. The British couldn't see that the Civil War was and had always been a war over slavery. And having so deeply misunderstood the full meaning of the war, they were unable to recognize any of the impressive antislavery policies already implemented by Lincoln and the Republicans. In her frustration with so much British confusion, Stowe went back to her desk and once again lifted her mighty pen—the pen that had already done so much to hasten slavery's demise. She would explain the Civil War to her British "sisters," but she would do it publicly, conspicuously, in an article for the January 1863 issue of the *Atlantic Monthly* magazine.[1]

In truth, the British and the Americans never really understood each other's position during the Civil War. Britons never fully appreciated the enduring effects of federalism and of the compromises the American Founders had made with slavery when they drafted a new Constitution in 1787. It had been nearly a century since an English judge, sitting on the Court of King's Bench, had ruled that when slaves set foot on English soil they ceased to be the property of their masters, setting in motion the disappearance of slavery from the island of England. Why, Britons wondered, were courts in the United States still protecting slavery rather than undermining it? It had been more than a generation since Parliament, by the mere passage of a statute, abolished slavery throughout the British Empire. Why couldn't Congress do the same thing in the United States?

Because most Americans—from the most radical opponents of slavery to the most extreme of slavery's defenders—took it for granted that the Constitution did not allow the federal government to interfere with slavery in the states where it existed. All antislavery politics started from that premise, but the British didn't really understand. So when Secretary of State William Seward told his British counterparts that the Union could not, constitutionally, prosecute a war for the purpose of abolishing slavery, the British mistakenly thought he was disavowing any desire to get slavery abolished. And when Lincoln said that his overriding purpose was to restore the Union, the British once again misread this as evidence that the president thought the war had nothing to do with slavery.

The misunderstanding went both ways. Northerners never understood that by recognizing the belligerent status of the Confederacy at the beginning of the war, Britain was actually aiding the Union. It meant that Britain would respect the northern embargo of southern ports. The Americans consistently misinterpreted the British move as evidence that they were itching to recognize the Confederacy itself when, in fact, supporters of the South—however vocal—were never in control of either Parliament or the ministry, In their frustration, Americans tried repeatedly to explain to the British why a war for the restoration of the Union was also a war about slavery.[2]

Obviously annoyed, Edward Everett dashed off a series of letters to the British foreign minister, Lord Russell, at the very beginning of the war. Everett had been both secretary of state and the minister to Great Britain and was on friendly terms with Russell, but he was upset by the speed with which England recognized the belligerent status of the Confederacy. In two 1861 letters, the first dated May 28 and the other August 19, Everett explained to Russell that Northerners were frustrated because they assumed Britain's anti-slavery bias would lead it to side naturally with the Union. "I cannot deny that we have been a little disappointed at the ground taken and the feeling indicated, on your side of the Water," Everett wrote. After all, "the controlling principle of the contest is the antagonism between slavery and anti-slavery. . . . Such being the case, we are disappointed in your readiness to recognize the Southern Confederacy as a belligerent power." In August Everett repeated his complaint that the "promptness" of Britain's recognition of the

Confederacy's belligerent status "was unexpected by us, in consideration of the antecedents of England on the subject of Slavery." But he went on to explain that "though the war is not, and could not under our Constitution be, waged for the abolition of Slavery, it does grow out of Slavery, and the Confederate government is by its Vice President declared to rest on Slavery as its Cornerstone."[3]

Eighteen months later Harriet Beecher Stowe was still fighting the same fight. She, too, assumed that the English were more supportive of the Confederacy than they actually were. Like Everett, she could not understand why Britain— having long since abolished slavery, having taken the lead in suppressing the slave trade—could sympathize with the slave republic that called itself the Confederate States of America. Stowe was willing to concede that in the earliest months of the war, when Edward Everett was trying to explain things to Lord Russell, it might not have seemed obvious to British observers that the Americans were engaged in a great struggle between freedom and slavery. But by November 1862 Stowe could point to a record of antislavery policies implemented by the North that left no more room for doubt. So she latched onto a pretext—a belated reply to an antislavery petition sent to America by half a million British women eight years earlier—to publish a full explanation of the true nature of America's Civil War.

Much had changed in the years since the petition was sent, Stowe explained. The slaveholders had tried and failed to grasp the levers of national power and spread slavery across the continent. The titanic struggle between slavery and freedom had come down, by 1860, to the simple question of whether slavery should be allowed to spread into the national territories. And when Abraham Lincoln's election signaled their defeat, the slaveholders "resolved to destroy the Union they could no longer control." They formed a Confederacy "which they openly declared to be the first republic founded on the right and determination of the white man to enslave the black man." Stowe reproduced lengthy extracts from the already notorious speech by the vice president of the Confederacy, Alexander Stephens, explaining why slavery was the "cornerstone" of the southern nation—the same speech Everett had pointed out to Lord Russell in 1861. The first thing British women needed to keep in mind in any reckoning of what the war was about, Stowe wrote, is why the southern states left the Union to begin with.

It was a necessary reminder, Stowe believed, because the slave states, having declared themselves an independent nation, were actively seeking "to secure the assistance of foreign powers." To that end the Southerners were taking "infinite pains . . . to blind and bewilder the mind of England as to the real issues of the conflict in America." This Confederate propaganda war had proven remarkably successful. "It has been often and earnestly asserted," Stowe complained, "that slavery had nothing to do with this conflict; that it was a mere struggle for power; that the only object was to restore the Union as it was; with all its abuses." This mythology was based, Stowe argued, on an almost willful misreading of the Confederate project and an equally serious misunderstanding of what Lincoln and the Republican Party stood for. The chief source of the misunderstanding was the familiar

Republican claim that they wanted to restore "the Union as it was." The British too often took this as evidence that the Republicans were content to restore the Union with slavery untouched. A fuller understanding of the party's position would dispel this misreading.

"It is the doctrine of the Republican party," Stowe explained, "that Freedom is national and Slavery sectional." Republicans believed that the Constitution "was designed for the promotion of liberty and not of slavery." Indeed, its framers "contemplated the gradual abolition of slavery." With an "antislavery majority" in control, federal power "could be so wielded as peaceably to extinguish this great evil." This was possible, Republicans reasoned, because slavery could not survive on its own without federal support. Slavery "ruins the land, and requires fresh territory for profitable working." It was also dangerous because slaves were invariably resentful and, given the chance, rebellious. "Slavery increases a dangerous population" and so required constant expansion to diffuse and defuse the threat. But what if the federal government were to bar it from the territories? "Slavery, then, being hemmed in by impassable limits, emancipation in each State becomes a necessity." Such was the doctrine of the Republican Party as Harriet Beecher Stowe understood it. It followed that by *restoring the Union as it was,* "the Republican party meant the Union in the sense contemplated by the original framers of it." That is to say, Republicans wanted to restore a "*status* in which, by the inevitable operation of natural laws, peaceful emancipation would become a certainty."

The record of the Republicans in power proved the depth of their commitment to slavery's destruction. It was but twelve months since the first regular session of the first Republican-controlled Congress had met in Washington and "proceeded to demonstrate the feasibility of overthrowing slavery by purely Constitutional measures." Not since the abolition of slavery in the West Indies had there been a "year more fruitful in anti-slavery triumphs." These included the abolition of slavery in the District of Columbia, a complete ban on slavery from all the western territories, and a "long-delayed treaty with Great Britain for the suppression of the slave-trade." Most significant of all, the president himself had "presented to the country a plan of peaceable emancipation with suitable compensation." This was an antislavery record so substantive and unambiguous that it was scarcely necessary to "infer" what Lincoln and his fellow Republicans meant by the restoration of "the Union as it was." The proof was in the deeds. By the exercise of the federal government's "normal Constitutional powers," Republicans believed, "slavery should be peaceably abolished."[4]

And yet, "this is but half the story of the anti-slavery triumphs of this year." For there was a second policy, military emancipation, which the Republicans were also implementing in hopes of bringing about slavery's destruction by means of "the Constitutional war-power." Though she wrote her essay in November 1862, a month before Lincoln issued an Emancipation Proclamation grounded in his power as commander in chief, the "Constitutional war-power" to free slaves had actually been in use for some time. "By this power," Stowe noted, it has already been decreed that "every slave of a Rebel who reaches the lines of our army becomes a free man; that all slaves found deserted by their masters become free men; that every slave employed in any service for the United States thereby obtains his liberty; and that every slave employed against the United States in any capacity obtains his liberty." To insure that the Union army conformed to this policy Congress had made it a crime for any officers to return any escaping slaves to their owners. With this statute, Stowe noted, "the Fugitive-Slave Law is for all present purposes practically repealed." As a result, "wherever our armies march, they carry liberty with them."

Military emancipation under the constitutional war power had already freed thousands of slaves by late 1862. Stowe cited the record of a single regiment that "to our certain knowledge liberated two thousand slaves during the past year, and this regiment is but one of hundreds." She pointed to the black soldiers, "recent refugees from slavery," already anxiously enlisting in the Union army in South Carolina and to the "free-labor experiment" already underway on the Sea Islands. "It is conceded on all sides, that, wherever our armies have had occupancy, there slavery has been practically abolished." Even President Lincoln acknowledged the fact. "Thus, even amid the roar of cannon and the confusion of war, cotton-planting, as a free-labor institution, is beginning its infant life, to grow hereafter to a glorious manhood." "Lastly," Stowe wrote, after all the antislavery "triumphs" that had already been achieved, "the great, decisive measure of the war" was about to appear, "*The President's Proclamation of Emancipation.*"

And yet this, too, "has been much misunderstood and misrepresented in England," Stowe complained. Cynical British critics were already insinuating that under the terms of Lincoln's forthcoming proclamation masters who were loyal to the Union were to be rewarded with the right to keep their slaves. To Stowe this reading of the proclamation could only be sustained by erasing the entire antislavery history of the war thus far. It was true that any state that returned voluntarily to the Union would be exempted from the Emancipation Proclamation, but they would be returning to a very different Union from the one they left:

> It is a Union which has abolished slavery in the District of Columbia, and interdicted slavery in the Territories,— which vigorously represses the slave-trade, and hangs the convicted slaver as a pirate,—which necessitates emancipation by denying expansion to slavery, and facilitates it by an offer of compensation. . . . The President's Proclamation simply means this: —Come in, and emancipate peaceably with compensation; stay out, and I emancipate, nor will I protect you from the consequences.

In Stowe's mind the two antislavery policies—state abolition and military emancipation—had become intertwined in a way that foreshadowed slavery's inevitable doom. The threat of military emancipation was becoming the decisive spur to the abolition of slavery in the states. Recent elections in Missouri and Delaware swept into office "strong majorities for emancipation. . . . Other States will soon follow," she predicted. There was no turning back. From the extraordinary antislavery achievements of the previous year, Stowe turned her gaze toward the future and drew a straight line to the destruction of slavery. It was not too much to hope, she wrote as 1863 approached, "that before a new year has gone far in its course the sacred fire of freedom will have flashed along the whole line of the Border States responsive to the generous proposition of the President and Congress, and that universal emancipation will have become a fixed fact in the American Union."

It diminishes not a whit of her exemplary achievement to point out that Harriet Beecher Stowe was a better historian than she was a seer. As early as November 1862 she was able to look back over the previous year to see all that had happened, put it in its proper context, and explain its significance. But she thought slavery would die more quickly, more easily, than it eventually did. She did not anticipate the limits of military emancipation, nor did she foresee the need for a constitutional amendment abolishing slavery. And yet there were glimmers of foresight in her prediction that the slave states themselves would begin to abolish slavery on their own. Her timing was off, but her insight was sound. The cordon of freedom might actually work—at least well enough so that by 1865 the balance of power between free and slave states would have shifted to a degree that made an abolition amendment at last conceivable.

It takes three-fourths of the states to ratify an amendment, but when the Civil War began there were fifteen slave and eighteen free states. An abolition amendment was out of the question. Nobody even imagined it. Why would they? Between 1804 and 1860 not a single state had abolished slavery. The point of the cordon of freedom was to restart the process, to pressure the slave states to begin abolishing slavery on their own. By the middle of 1862 Lincoln and the

Republicans in Congress had built their cordon. They had banned slavery from the territories, abolished it in Washington, stopped enforcing the fugitive slave clause almost everywhere, begun to suppress slavery on the high seas, and they were not allowing any new slave states into the Union. But just as the mainstream practice of wartime emancipation was radicalized by war when it was extended to millions of slaves, so was the cordon of freedom radicalized by war. In 1862 Lincoln began to warn the Border States that if they did not abolish it on their own slavery would be undermined by the "friction and abrasion" of war. A year later his administration began actively enlisting tens of thousands of Border State slaves into the Union Army, promising freedom to them and their families in return for military service. By 1864 it was Union policy to require seceded states to abolish slavery as a condition for readmission to the Union. These policies dramatically altered the balance of power between slave and free states. After half a century of inaction, state abolition suddenly resumed. By the time the war ended five states had abolished slavery, West Virginia had been admitted to the Union only on condition that it abolish slavery, and two new free states were added as well. By early 1865 there were twenty-six free states and only ten slave states. Abolition in one more state would create a Union in which three-fourths of the states were free. By the time the House of Representatives sent the Thirteenth Amendment to the states for ratification in January of 1865, the scorpion was poised to administer its last, lethal sting.

Acknowledgments

Three of the four chapters were written in response to an invitation to deliver the Walter Lynwood Fleming Lectures at Louisiana State University, so my first debt of gratitude is to the faculty and graduate students at the LSU History Department for their cordial and friendly reception and for several days of pleasant intellectual stimulation. Special thanks to Victor Stater for steering me through the arrangements and for being such a gracious host, and to Bill Cooper and Gaines Foster for pushing me to clarify or modify points that needed both. For reading the chapters and offering helpful comments, thanks to Joe Murphy, John Blanton, Greg Downs, Eric Foner, Bruce Levine, John Stauffer, and Steve Forman. John Stauffer located several remarkable images of the scorpion's sting, one of which now graces the cover of this book. Graham Peck and Rod Davis provided me with some of the sources I cite. Burruss Carnahan responded to an e-mail from a complete stranger by reading and editing an earlier version of chapter four. That there is a later version is due primarily to my friend, John Witt, whose critical reading was both detailed and, given our differences, uncommonly gracious.

.

Notes

Introduction: At Stake

1. James Oakes, *Freedom National: The Destruction of Slavery in the United States, 1861–1865* (New York, 2013).

Chapter 1: "Like a Scorpion Girt by Fire"

1. *Congressional Globe*, 36th Cong., 1st sess., p. 586.
2. Ibid.
3. *Fifteenth Annual Report, Presented to the Massachusetts Anti-Slavery Society, by Its Board of Managers* (Boston, 1847), p. 56.
4. Andrew Dickson White, *The Doctrines and Policy of the Republican Party: As Given by Its Recognized Leaders, Orators, Presses, and Platforms* (Washington, D.C., 1860), p. 3.
5. James Redpath, *A Guide to Hayti* (Boston, 1861), p. 10.
6. James Freeman Clarke, *Causes and Consequences of the Affair at Harper's Ferry: A Sermon Preached in the Indiana Place Chapel, on Sunday Morning, Nov. 6, 1859* (Boston, 1859), p. 9.
7. William M. French, ed., *Life, Speeches, State Papers and Public Services of Gov. Oliver P. Morton* (Cincinnati, 1864), p. 46.
8. Arthur Schlesinger Jr., ed., *History of American Presidential Elections, 1848–1896* vol. 2 (New York, 1971), p. 1126.

9. *Jacksonville (Ill.) Morgan Journal,* Oct. 19, 1854. See also Ottawa (Ill.) *Register,* Oct. 14, 1854.

10. Roy P. Basler, ed., *Collected Works of Abraham Lincoln* [hereafter *CW*] (New Brunswick, N.J., 1953–1955), vol. 3, p. 4.

11. Schlesinger, ed., *History of American Presidential Elections,* vol. 2, p. 1126.

12. Thomas Morris, *Free Men All: The Personal Liberty Laws of the North, 1780–1861* (Baltimore, 1974).

13. Paul Finkelman, *An Imperfect Union: Slavery, Federalism, and Comity* (Chapel Hill, N.C., 1981).

14. *New York Times,* Oct. 15, 1855.

15. Carl Schurz, *Speeches of Carl Schurz* (Philadelphia, 1865), pp. 26, 33–36. From "The Irrepressible Conflict," delivered at Mechanics Hall in Chicago, Sept. 28, 1858.

16. Ibid., p. 36.

17. John A. Gilmer to Abraham Lincoln, Dec. 10, 1860, *Abraham Lincoln Papers, Library of Congress;* Lincoln's reply to Gilmer is in *CW,* vol. 4, pp. 151ff.

18. *Cong. Globe,* 37th Cong., 2nd sess., p. 1340.

19. *Cong. Globe,* 36th Cong., 2nd sess., pp. 112ff.

20. A few days before Crittenden introduced his proposal, Andrew Johnson of Tennessee introduced a similar set of constitutional revisions as a basis for sectional reconciliation. The major difference was Johnson's willingness to repeal all federal legislation regarding fugitive slaves, making it "the duty of each state" to enforce the fugitive slave clause. *Cong. Globe,* 36th Cong., 2nd sess., p. 83.

21. *Cong. Globe,* 36th Cong., 2nd sess., pp. 99ff.

22. Ibid., pp. 101–2.

23. Trusten Polk, "The Crisis, and What It Demands!" Speech of Hon. T. Polk, of Missouri, Delivered in the Senate of the United States, Jan. 14, 1861 (Washington D.C., 1861), p. 8.

24. Robert Augustus Toombs, Speech of Hon. Robert Toombs, on the Crisis: Delivered before the Georgia Legislature, Dec. 7, 1860 (Washington D.C., 1860), p. 8.

25. *Cong. Globe,* 36th Cong., 2nd sess., p. 240. The widespread secessionist fear of slavery's strangulation by encirclement has been

amply documented in a number of works by William W. Freehling, *The Road to Disunion, Volume I: Secessionists at Bay, 1776–1854*
(New York, 1990); *The Reintegration of American History: Slavery and
the Civil War* (New York, 1994); and *The Road to Disunion, Volume
II: Secessionists Triumphant, 1854–1861* (New York, 2007).

Chapter 2: The Right versus the Wrong of Property in Man

1. Quoted in Bernard Bailyn, *The Ideological Origins of the American
   Revolution* (Cambridge, Mass., 1967), pp. 232–33.
2. James L. Huston, *Calculating the Value of the Union: Slavery, Property
   Rights, and the Economic Origins of the Civil War* (Chapel Hill, N.C.,
   2003), p. 14.
3. Elizabeth Cady Stanton, *Address to the Legislature of New York Adopted
   by the State Woman's Rights Convention . . .* (Albany, N.Y., 1854), p. 9.
4. Carl Schurz, *Speeches of Carl Schurz* (Philadelphia, 1865), p. 126.
5. *Congressional Globe,* 24th Cong., 2nd sess., p. 159.
6. Orlando Patterson, *Slavery and Social Death: A Comparative Study*
   (Cambridge, Mass., 1982), catalogs some two hundred different
   forms of slavery in world history.
7. David Brion Davis, *The Problem of Slavery in the Age of Revolution,
   1770–1823,* 2nd ed. (New York, 1999), p. 39. Davis reaffirmed the
   significance of "property" in Davis, *Inhuman Bondage: The Rise and
   Fall of Slavery in the New World* (New York, 2006), p. 32. M. I. Finley,
   Ancient Slavery and Modern Ideology (New York, 1980), pp. 67–73;
   Claude Meillasoux, *The Anthropology of Slavery: The Womb of Iron
   and Gold* (Chicago, 1991), pp. 11, 14.
8. Huston, *Calculating the Value of the Union,* p. 22.
9. Ibid., pp. 51–52.
10. http://www.kansasmemory.org/item/207409/text.
11. James Oakes, *Freedom National: The Destruction of Slavery in the
    United States, 1861–1865* (New York, 2013), p. 452.
12. Chesapeake slavery certainly evolved over the course of the sev-
    enteenth century. In the earliest decades the institution had
    many of the more malleable attributes of slavery in other soci-
    eties: not only were slaves manumitted more often; once freed
    they often became slaveholders themselves. By 1700, however,

Chesapeake slavery had taken on the familiar attributes of Anglo-American slavery: the master's property right was more absolute, and few slaves were manumitted.

This is not to suggest that slavery could flourish without many laws that, among other things, stipulated who could be enslaved, regulated the policing of slaves, and determined the disposition of slave property upon the death or financial distress of the master. But these statutes assumed that slavery already existed. They did not *create* slavery so much as they regulated it.

Curiously, Massachusetts established slavery in 1641 as an exception to a general rule banning it: "There shall never be any bond slavery, villinage or captivitie amongst us unles it be lawful captives taken in just warres, and such strangers as willingly sell themselves or are sold to us." Quoted in George H. Moore, *Notes on the History of Slavery in Massachusetts* (Boston, 1866), p. 12.

13. Huston, *Calculating the Value of the Union*, p. 16. On the significance of self-ownership, see C. B. Macpherson, *The Political Theory of Possessive Individualism* (Oxford, 1962), pp. 137–42.

14. Henry Wilson, *History of the Rise and Fall of the Slave Power*, vol. 1 (1874), pp. 300–301.

15. *Register of Debates*, 20th Cong., 2nd sess., p. 167.

16. Ibid., pp. 175–81. In the laws governing the cession of land by Maryland and Virginia to form the District, it was provided that the laws of those states would remain in force in the relevant parts of the District. Thus, if Virginia law assumed a black was a slave, so must D.C. law.

17. Ibid., pp. 181–87.

18. *Remarks of Mr. Hammond, of South Carolina, on the Question of Receiving the Petitions for the Abolition of Slavery in the District of Columbia* (Washington, D.C., 1836), p. 4.

19. Theodore Dwight Weld, *The Power of Congress over Slavery in the District of Columbia* (New York, 1838), pp. 13, 39, 41–43. For political context, see Jacobus tenBroek, *Equal under Law* (New York, 1965), pp. 21–23; William M. Wiecek, *The Sources of Antislavery Constitutionalism in America, 1760–1848* (Ithaca, N.Y., 1977), pp. 189–91; Helen Knowles, "Slavery and the Constitution: A Special Relationship," *Slavery & Abolition* 28 (2007): 309–28.

On Weld's role in the antislavery movement, see Gilbert Hobbs Barnes, *The Antislavery Impulse: 1830–1844* (New York, 1933); Benjamin P. Thomas, *Theodore Weld, Crusader for Freedom* (New Brunswick, N.J., 1950); James M. McPherson, "The Fight against the Gag Rule: Joshua Leavitt and Antislavery Insurgency in the Whig Party, 1839–1842," *The Journal of Negro History* 48 (July, 1963): 188–95.

20. Wilson, *Rise and Fall of the Slave Power,* vol. 1, pp. 473–74.
21. Ibid., pp. 474–75.
22. *Cong. Globe,* 30th Cong., 1st sess., p. 876.
23. Roy P. Basler, ed., *Collected Works of Abraham Lincoln* (New Brunswick, N.J., 1953–1955), vol. 4, pp. 1–7.

Chapter 3: Race Conflict

1. *Memphis Daily Appeal,* Nov. 30, 1858.
2. Roy P. Basler, ed., *Collected Works of Abraham Lincoln* [hereafter *CW*], (New Brunswick, N.J., 1953–1955), vol. 4, pp. 19–20.
3. James Oakes, "Natural Rights, Citizenship Rights, States' Rights, and Black Rights: Another Look at Lincoln and Race," in Eric Foner, ed., *Our Lincoln: New Perspectives on Lincoln and His World* (New York, 2008), pp. 109–34.
4. Rodney O. Davis and Douglas L. Wilson, *The Lincoln-Douglas Debates: The Lincoln Studies Center Edition* (Urbana, Ill., 2008), p. 131. Like many Republicans, Lincoln's views on race evolved over the course of the war, and just before his assassination he openly endorsed a limited form of black suffrage—the first president to do so. On Lincoln's "radicalization" during the war, see James Oakes, *The Radical and the Republican: Frederick Douglass, Abraham Lincoln, and the Triumph of Antislavery Politics* (New York, 2007), and Eric Foner, *The Fiery Trial: Abraham Lincoln and American Slavery* (New York, 2010). Michael Burlingame, *Abraham Lincoln: A Life* (Baltimore, 2008), vol. 2, pp. 810–16, presents compelling evidence that John Wilkes Booth assassinated Lincoln *because* of his endorsement of black suffrage.
5. *CW,* vol. 2, pp. 265–66.
6. *CW,* vol. 2, pp. 519–20.

7. *CW,* vol. 3, pp. 9–10.

8. *CW,* vol. 2, p. 409.

9. *CW,* vol. 4, p. 16.

10. Jon L. Wakelyn, ed., *Southern Pamphlets on Secession, November 1860–April 1861* (Chapel Hill, N.C., 1996), pp. 37–38.

11. Charles Francis Adams, *An Oration, Delivered before the Municipal Authorities of the City of Fall River, July 4, 1860* (Fall River, Mass., 1860).

12. Arthur Schlesinger Jr., ed., *History of American Presidential Elections, 1848–1896* vol. 2 (New York, 1971), p. 1126.

13. Henry Wilson, *History of the Rise and Fall of the Slave Power,* vol. 1 (Boston, 1874), pp. 154–55.

14. Ibid., p. 156.

15. *Annals of Congress,* Senate, 16th Cong., 2nd sess., p. 94.

16. Ibid., pp. 454, 508–17.

17. Ibid., pp. 524, 525, 529–30.

18. Wilson, *Rise and Fall of the Slave Power,* vol. 1, pp. 576–86.

19. On the Negro-Seamen Act, see William W. Freehling, *Prelude to Civil War: The Nullification Controversy in South Carolina, 1816–1836* (New York, 1965), pp. 111–16; William M. Wiecek, *The Sources of Antislavery Constitutionalism in America, 1760–1848* (Ithaca, N.Y., 1977), p. 139; Harold Melvin Hyman and William M. Wiecek, *Equal Justice under Law: Constitutional Development, 1835–1875* (New York, 1982), pp. 79–81.

20. *CW,* vol. 2, p. 256. See also Leslie Friedman Goldstein, "A 'Triumph of Freedom' After All?: *Prigg v. Pennsylvania* Re-Examined," *Law and History Review* 29, no. 3 (August 2011): 763–96.

21. Quoted in Thomas D. Morris, *Southern Slavery and the Law, 1619–1860* (Chapel Hill, N.C., 1996), p. 372.

22. *Dred Scott v. Sandford,* 60 U.S. 393 (1856).

23. *CW,* vol. 2, p. 403.

24. Ibid., p. 453.

25. Ibid.

26. Ibid., pp. 462, 464.

27. Ibid., pp. 3, 9.

28. Ibid., pp. 3, 112.

29. *CW,* vol. 4, pp. 262–71.

30. *Congressional Globe,* 36th Cong., 2nd sess., p. 356.

31. *A Declaration of the Immediate Causes which Induce and Justify the Secession of Georgia from the Federal Union* (Washington, D.C., 2009).

32. *A Declaration of the Immediate Causes which Induce and Justify the Secession of the State of Mississippi from the Federal Union* (Jackson, Miss., 1861), p. 4.

33. *A Declaration of the Immediate Causes which Induce and Justify the Secession of South Carolina from the Federal Union* (Charleston, S.C., 1860), p. 10.

34. *A Declaration of the Causes which Impelled the State of Texas to Secede from the Union* (Austin, Tex., 1861).

Chapter 4: The Wars over Wartime Emancipation

1. See, for example, Thaddeus Stevens's defense of military emancipation under the law of nations in *Congressional Globe,* 37th Cong., 1st sess., p. 414.

2. "Circular" to the governors of the Confederate states, Nov. 26, 1862, in *Jefferson Davis, Constitutionalist: His Letters, Papers, and Speeches,* ed. Dunbar Rowland, vol. 5 (Jackson, Miss., 1923), p. 277.

3. On the number of slaves escaping to the British, see Allan Kulikoff, "Uprooted Peoples: Black Migrants in the Age of the American Revolution, 1790–1820," in Ira Berlin and Ronald Hoffman, eds., *Slavery and Freedom in the Age of the American Revolution* (Urbana, Ill., 1983), pp. 144–45; Cassandra Pybus, "Jefferson's Faulty Math: The Question of Slave Defections in the American Revolution," *William and Mary Quarterly,* 3d ser., 62 (April, 2005): 243–64. On the fate of black loyalists generally, see Maya Jasanoff, *Liberty's Exiles: American Loyalists in a Revolutionary World* (New York, 2011).

4. The South Carolina legislature balked. Rather than free slaves in return for military service, it offered to *give* a slave as an enlistment bounty to any white man who joined the Continental army. American and British policies were not identical. When the British emancipated enemy slaves, the freed people had to leave the country or risk reenslavement when the war ended. Their masters were never compensated. But because the Americans were

freeing their own slaves, they compensated the masters, and the slaves themselves, having been legally purchased, could safely return to their own homes as free men at war's end.

5. Arming slaves in wartime was a firmly established tradition throughout world history. See Philip D. Morgan and Andrew Jackson O'Shaughnessy, "Arming Slaves in the American Revolution," in Christopher Leslie Brown and Philip D. Morgan, eds., *Arming Slaves: From Classical Times to the Modern Age* (New Haven, 2006), pp. 180–208; Eliga H. Gould, *Among the Powers of the Earth: The American Revolution and the Making of a New World Empire* (Cambridge, Mass., 2012), pp. 71–78.

6. As several scholars have noted, Mansfield's actual decision was far more ambiguous than the principle that bore the name "Somerset." See, for example, William M. Wiecek, "Somerset: Lord Mansfield and the Legitimacy of Slavery in the Anglo-American World," *University of Chicago Law Review* vol. 42, no. 1 (Autumn 1974): 86–146; David Brion Davis, *The Problem of Slavery in the Age of Revolution* (Ithaca, N.Y., 1975), and George Van Cleve, *A Slaveholders' Union: Slavery, Politics, and the Constitution in the Early American Republic* (Chicago, 2010).

7. On the crucial importance of treaties in the late eighteenth century, see Gould, *Among the Powers of the Earth.*

8. *The Public Statutes at Large of the United States of America . . . ,* vol. 8 (Boston, 1846), p. 83.

9. Benjamin Quarles, *The Negro in the American Revolution* (Chapel Hill, N.C., 1961), p. 165.

10. *Journal of the Continental Congress,* vol. 24, pp. 242–43.

11. Christopher Leslie Brown, *Moral Capital: Foundations of British Abolitionism* (Chapel Hill, N.C., 2006), pp. 298–300. Black loyalists freed by the British were not reenslaved, as American propagandists charged, but they were not treated all that well either. See Jasanoff, *Liberty's Exiles.*

12. *Journal of the Continental Congress,* vol. 31, pp. 864–65.

13. Ibid., pp. 865–66. Jay would shortly become president of the New York Manumission Society.

14. John Jay to Edmund Randolph, Sept. 13, 1794, in *American State Papers* [*hereafter ASP*], *Foreign Relations,* vol. 1, p. 485.

15. Randolph to Jay, Dec. 3, 1794, *ASP,* pp. 509ff.

16. Ibid.

17. John Jay to Edmund Randolph, February 6, 1795, *ASP,* p. 518.

18. *Remarks on the Treaty of Amity, Commerce, and Navigation, Made between the United States and Great Britain,* in Harold C. Syrett, ed., *The Papers of Alexander Hamilton,* vol. 18 (Charlottesville, Va., 2011), pp. 415–16.

19. Ibid., pp. 416–17.

20. Ibid., pp. 518–21, in "The Defence No. III," July 29, 1795. By all appearances Hamilton was well versed in Enlightenment theories of the law of nations. Having cited Vattel and Grotius in his memo to Washington, Hamilton now cited Blackstone's dictum that "a slave or negro, the instant he lands in England, becomes a freeman," and Pufendorf's claim that if the relation of master and slave is "broken by war," the master's right to the slave becomes "extinct" and the slave's "natural liberty returns."

21. Ibid.

22. The mere fact that there *was* a debate in the House of Representatives was controversial. The Senate had approved Jay's treaty and Washington had long since ratified it. Under the Constitution the House had no formal role in the treaty-making process. So the congressmen spent nearly all of March 1796 arguing over whether it was any of the House's business to be arguing over the treaty. When President Washington finally refused a House request for documentation of the treaty-making process, on the grounds that the request was unconstitutional, opponents of the treaty shifted ground by claiming that the House could refuse to authorize the funds necessary to implement the treaty. This was the resolution that sparked a monthlong debate over the strengths and weaknesses of the treaty itself. The debate over whether the House had any business debating the treaty takes up more than 350 pages in *Annals of Congress,* 4th Cong., 1st sess., pp. 426–783.

23. *Annals of Congress,* 4th Cong., 1st sess., pp. 771, 978.

24. Ibid., p. 977.

25. See, for example, ibid., pp. 1005–6.

26. Ibid., p. 1018.

27. See, for example, ibid., pp. 1070–71.

28. Ibid., p. 1106.
29. Ibid., p. 1143.
30. Ibid., pp. 1078–79.
31. Ibid., pp. 1080–84.
32. Ibid., p. 1084. Emphasis added.
33. Ibid., pp. 1084–85.
34. See, for example, ibid., pp. 1027–28.
35. Ibid., p. 1062.
36. Ibid., p. 1232–33.
37. Ibid., pp. 1123, 1185.
38. Ibid., pp. 1142–43, 1177.
39. Ibid., p. 1223.
40. Ibid., pp. 1131–32.
41. Ibid., p. 1291.
42. For a different view, see John Fabian Witt, *Lincoln's Code: The Laws of War in American History* (New York, 2012). Witt argues that before the Civil War Hamilton was the only American statesman to defend military emancipation under the laws of war and that in so doing Hamilton relied on medieval "just war" theories rather than Enlightenment writers such as Vattel and Grotius.
43. *ASP, Foreign Relations,* vol. 3, 13th Cong., 3rd sess., p. 746.
44. *ASP, Foreign Relations,* vol. 4, 14th Cong., 2nd sess., p. 114.
45. Ibid., pp. 106–7.
46. Ibid., p. 108.
47. Ibid., p. 110.
48. Ibid., p. 113. The best account of these events is Alan Taylor, *The Internal Enemy: Slavery and War in Virginia, 1772–1832* (New York, 2013).
49. *ASP, Foreign Relations,* vol. 4, 14th Cong., 2nd sess., pp. 111ff.
50. Ibid., p. 117.
51. Ibid., pp. 125–26.
52. Ibid., pp. 116–17. Adams's blanket denial of a belligerent's right to emancipate enemy slaves was inconsistent with the position taken by all American statesmen during the Jay treaty debates of the 1790s. He never denied that slaves could take advantage of a war by emancipating *themselves*—as opposed to being freed by the enemy.

53. Ibid., p. 117. As Adams reported the British position on August 22, 1815, "There were, perhaps, few or no slaves in the places then occupied by them [along the eastern seaboard], but there was a probability, at the time when the treaty was signed, that New Orleans and other parts of the southern States might be in their possession at the time of the exchange of ratifications."

54. *ASP, Foreign Relations,* vol. 5, 17th Cong., 2nd sess., pp. 214, 220.

55. Ibid., p. 221.

56. *ASP, Foreign Relations,* vol. 6, 19th Cong., 2nd sess., pp. 331–55. The text of the final convention negotiated by Gallatin is on p. 355.

57. Ibid., p. 342.

58. Ibid.

59. Ibid., pp. 855–57.

60. Ibid., pp. 883ff.

61. *ASP, Foreign Relations,* vol. 5, p. 220.

62. *ASP, Military Affairs,* vol. 7, p. 821.

63. Joshua Giddings, *The Exiles of Florida, or, the Crimes Committed by Our Government against the Maroons* . . . (Columbus, Ohio, 1858), p. 140.

64. Ibid., p. 143.

65. Ibid, pp. 144ff.

66. William Whiting, *The War Powers of the President, Military Arrests, and Reconstruction of the Union,* 8th ed. (Boston, 1864), pp. 75–76.

67. *Cong. Globe,* 24th Cong., 1st sess., p. 499.

68. Ibid., appendix, p. 448.

69. Ibid.

70. Ibid.

71. Ibid., p. 450.

72. *Cong. Globe,* 27th Cong., 1st sess., p. 342.

73. *Private and Official Correspondence of Gen. Benjamin G. Butler,* vol. 1 (Norwood, Mass., 1917), pp. 185–88.

74. Roy P. Basler, ed., *Collected Works of Abraham Lincoln* [hereafter *CW*] (New Brunswick, N.J., 1953–1955), vol. 7, p. 51.

75. *General Orders No. 100: Instructions for the Government of Armies of the United States in the Field,* Sec. 1, Arts, pp. 42–43.

76. Dunbar Rowland, ed., *Jefferson Davis: Constitutionalist,* vol. 5 (New York, 1923), pp. 392–93.

77. Ibid., p. 409.
78. *The War of the Rebellion: A Compilation of the Official Records of the War of the Union and Confederate Armies* (Washington, D.C., 1880–1901), ser. 2, vol. 6, pp. 42–43.
79. Ibid., pp. 44–45.
80. For a different view, see Witt, *Lincoln's Code,* p. 263. "By insisting on nondiscrimination" in the way Confederates treated black and white soldiers, Witt writes, Lieber's code of war "had a hand in the greatest humanitarian disaster of the last two years of the war. Some 55,000 men died in Civil War prison camps. Had exchanges been allowed to go forward on the South's terms, countless of those men would have lived." It is also true, of course, had the Confederates not insisted on reenslaving black soldiers, "countless of those men would have lived." But Witt seems to assume that reenslaving black prisoners by the Confederates was consistent with the morally neutral principles of enlightened warfare, whereas the Union's demand for "nondiscrimination" represented a reversion to the medieval principle of "just war." This distinction follows logically from Witt's remarkable claim that military emancipation itself was a "startling departure from the spirit of the eighteenth-century laws of war." However, the evidence presented in these pages indicates that military emancipation was considered legitimate by nearly all British and American leaders and that reenslavement was at best controversial and was often denounced as an "odious" and "infamous" departure from the enlightened rules of war. What was unprecedented about the Union war effort was not military emancipation as such, but universal military emancipation with the goal of abolishing slavery entirely. Whether that was a violation or a fulfillment of Enlightenment principles is an interesting question.
81. *CW,* vol. 6, p. 176.

Epilogue: Harriet Beecher Stowe and Her British Sisters

1. Harriet Beecher Stowe, "A Reply to the Address of the Women of England," *Atlantic Monthly* 11, no. 63 (Jan., 1863), pp. 120–34.
2. Howard Jones, *Blue and Gray Diplomacy: A History of Union and*

Confederate Foreign Relations (Chapel Hill, N.C., 2010), is particularly insightful about how deeply the British and the Americans misunderstood each other's position.

3. Edward Everett to Lord John Russell, May 28 and August 19, 1861, British National Archives, Public Record Office 30/22/39.

4. Stowe acknowledged that there were some abolitionists who believed the federal government could go even further, but she claimed—a bit disingenuously—to be less interested in arguing the merits of the Republican position than in explaining just what that position was.

Index